Bonjour, Happiness!

Sonya,
May you discover
your "inner French Girl"!
Enjoy,
Adrienne

BOOKS BY JAMIE CAT CALLAN

Bonjour, Happiness!

French Women Don't Sleep Alone

Bonjour, Happiness!

SECRETS TO FINDING YOUR *JOIE DE VIVRE*

JAMIE CAT CALLAN

CITADEL PRESS
Kensington Publishing Corp.
www.kensingtonbooks.com

CITADEL PRESS BOOKS are published by

Kensington Publishing Corp.
119 West 40th Street
New York, NY 10018

All Kensington titles, imprints, and distributed lines are available at special quantity discounts for bulk purchases for sales promotions, premiums, fund-raising, educational, or institutional use. Special book excerpts or customized printings can also be created to fit specific needs. For details, write or phone the office of the Kensington special sales manager: Kensington Publishing Corp., 119 West 40th Street, New York, NY 10018, attn: Special Sales Department; phone 1-800-221-2647.

CITADEL PRESS and the Citadel logo are Reg. U.S. Pat. & TM Off.

First printing: April 2011

10 9 8 7 6 5 4 3

Printed in the United States of America

Library of Congress Control Number: 2010931897

ISBN-13: 978-0-8065-3410-7
ISBN-10: 0-8065-3410-9

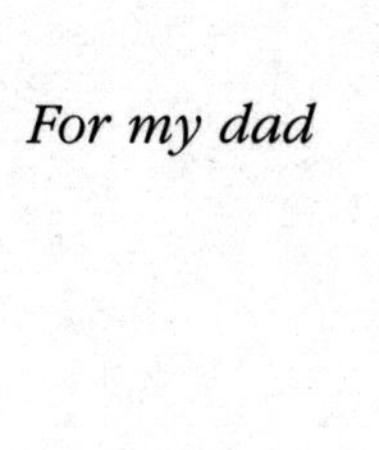

For my dad

La bonheur le plus doux est celui qu'on partage.

(The sweetest happiness is the one that we share.)

—Old French proverb

Contents

Bonjour, Happiness!

INTRODUCTION

MY GRANDMOTHER WAS FRENCH.

She was French in a way that I will never be—no matter how hard I try. And believe me, I've tried.

My maternal grandmother was strikingly beautiful. She was tall and slender and dark. She tanned easily and before her hair turned silver, it was jet black. She liked to wear it in sleek 1930s-style waves. My mother and I looked nothing like her. We were not tall. We were not slim. We were blondes with blue eyes, and with . . . well, plenty of curves.

To my family, especially to my father's Irish side, and indeed to our friends and neighbors, my grandmother was extremely exotic, even mesmerizing. She spoke with a slight accent, left over from a childhood where she and her brothers and sisters spoke only French at home and didn't learn English until they began grammar school. My mother tried to be "French" in her own way. Occasionally, while I was growing up, she'd tell me *fermez la bouche!* (meaning "shut your mouth!") and every now and then my mother would take a break from cooking frozen Swanson TV dinners and attempt a French béchamel sauce, with butter, flour, and milk. She would mix the ingredients in a saucepan, adding canned Bumble Bee tuna, and then she would serve this—smothered in a layer of black pepper—over toasted Wonder Bread. When my brother and I complained that it was too hot, she'd tell us, "I can't help it! I'm French! I like spices—not like you cold Irish people!"

I have no idea where she got the idea that the French like to overpepper their food. Or for that matter, that the Irish are "cold." (Perhaps she was talking about my father, who was not cold, but kept quiet around her, for his own good.)

My mother could be very theatrical. She was petite and girlish, but she could also be very provocative—kind of like a doll with a dirty mouth. She was used to getting a lot of attention and I think this made growing older all the more difficult for her. And when she found the power of her attractiveness waning in her forties and fifties, she became downright despondent.

This was not the case for my grandmother, who was elegant and stylish and quite stunning well into her eighties. In fact, I have photographs that my grandfather took of my grandmother while they were in Florida during the winter months. In one black-and-white photograph, she is standing in a yard in front of some bird of paradise flowers, wearing a one-piece bathing suit. She stands with perfect posture, one leg turned in front of the other, so that she is looking out from a slight angle. Her hair is wet, slicked back, and there are a few damp curls creeping around her ears. She doesn't look directly at the camera's eye, but rather she is looking away into the not-too-far distance, as if she has better things to do than to be photographed in her bathing suit. Her wry smile says, *Yes, I know you find me beautiful. I know I am tall and slender. I know you think I am a bathing beauty, but really, enough of this now!* But, my grandfather, who was crazy in love with her, couldn't help but take many such photographs. They had a very steamy marriage. That was obvious.

My grandmother certainly knew the secret to *joie de vivre.* No, she didn't tell wild jokes or risqué stories or tap dance around the kitchen (all of which my mother did), but rather, in her own quiet way, she found balance, joy, and *l'art de vivre* (the art of living). She gardened, she jarred fresh fruits and vegetables from my grandparents' little farm and later from their own backyard. She composted and recycled long before it became fashionable. She fished and actually hunted with my grandfather. She sewed clothes for us. I'll never forget how she took her old fur coat from the 1940s that was beyond repair and cut it up to make matching Jackie Kennedy-style hats and little fur collars for me, my mother, and for herself. She didn't give us big, expensive gifts, but whatever she gave, you could be sure it was from the heart. She loved consignment shops and thrift stores. She loved the thrill of the hunt and the joy of finding something old and beautiful, but forgotten and discarded—something that she could rescue and rediscover.

During her Sunday afternoon visits, she would often shampoo and curl my hair. This was, in part, my mother's idea. My mother, who loved Shirley Temple and taught tap-dancing lessons, had introduced me to her old black-and-white movies—*Curly Top, Baby Take a Bow, The Little Princess, Captain January, Rebecca of Sunnybrook Farm.* And she told me that I could look just like Shirley Temple if only we could get my hair done up into a bunch of those bouncy little ringlets.

And so, my grandmother arrived and went straight to work. She gave me a shampoo in our upstairs bathroom, with me standing on a little step stool, my head bowed over the sink as she worked the fragrant bubbles through my hair and rinsed it gently. I loved the feeling of her fingers at the nape of my neck, and the warm water flowing over my head.

Once my hair was towel dried and combed, I sat in a chair, while she twirled the damp pieces of my hair around small strips of cloth that she had fashioned out of old sheets. All this effort, so that I could go to school on Monday with a head full of Shirley Temple ringlets, or "rag curls," as she called them.

By the sixth grade, the Beatles were all the rage and the girls in my school were all straightening their hair, but I still wanted my grandmother to curl my hair on Sundays, not so much for the ringlets—which didn't even last through all of Monday—but for the experience of having her gentle hands slowly rinsing my hair in warm water. I loved how she took her time, carefully tying up the curls and how she smiled at me in the reflected mirror.

I OFTEN THINK of my grandmother nowadays—not simply because I am writing books about Frenchwomen, but because I am no longer "a spring chicken." In fact, I'm fifty-six. I'm the mother of a twenty-six-year-old daughter. I divorced my first husband in 1994 and remarried in 2005.

Yet, even with a wonderful husband and a career I thoroughly enjoy, I am full of insecurities about my looks, my clothes, and my ever expanding, then contracting, then expanding again waistline. I worry about money. I struggle with the balance between work-work-work and having fun and enjoying my free time. I often feel that I was not a good enough mother to my daughter. I often sense that I lack a certain balance in my life. Sometimes my husband will return home from his work to find me still in my nightgown, still hunched over my computer, and he'll say, "You are exactly where I left you this morning—you must go out and get some fresh air!"

I am a woman who often feels that I am not smart enough, not rich enough, not organized enough, not accomplished enough, not slim enough, and definitely not *young* enough.

All this is to say I'm a typical American gal!

And I know I am not alone in these feelings. When I wrote *French Women Don't Sleep Alone* I traveled all over France with my good friend and translator, Jessica Lee, interviewing hundreds of women (and lots of men, too) and later on my own I traveled throughout the United States where I talked to hundreds more. I came to realize that as American women we have much to learn from our French sisters—yes, about love, romance, and marriage, but also about everyday living, shopping, buying fresh food, about the simple joys of being alive, appreciating what life has to offer us right now, in this moment—no matter what our age or shape or size or how much money we have in our pocketbooks. With their philosophy of "working to live" rather than "living to work," Frenchwomen know a thing or two about balance. And I believe that they can teach us something about how we might at least start to finally feel that we are "enough."

I decided to return to France on this quest to discover the secret to *joie de vivre*. But since I have very limited funds,

I applied for a Virginia Center for the Creative Arts fellowship to live and work in Auvillar, a little village in the southwest of France. I will always be indebted to the Virginia Center for the Creative Arts and to the village of Auvillar, France, for welcoming me so warmly and offering a dream come true: a home base in France.

During my journeys, I have talked to Frenchwomen from all socio-economic groups, urban and rural, old and young and somewhere in the middle. I've tracked down those gorgeous *femmes d'un certain âge* and asked them how they stay so elegant and so confident into their fifties, sixties, seventies, and beyond. I've attended more dinner parties than I can count. I've attended cooking classes and I've helped organize French dinner parties—from elaborate fêtes to simple, spontaneous potluck get-togethers and everything in between.

I've interviewed all sorts of Frenchwomen—beautiful and not so beautiful, slim and not so slim, well-to-do and not so well-to-do. I found women in the countryside, tiny villages in the Southwest, the northern provinces, the coastal resort towns, the cities (Paris, *bien sûr*!), Toulouse, Lille, Besançon, Dijon, Lyon, and the suburbs. I talked to university students, housewives, office workers, doctors, lawyers, bakers, shop owners, photographers, and artists. I talked to a woman who makes her own artisan soap, a librarian, several beauticians and estheticians, an image consultant, business executives, a few health care professionals, and many others. Some of these meetings were casual and some were more formal interviews. I got into conversations wherever I happened to be at any given time. In Auvillar where I lived for a month, I helped harvest grapes for wine with my fellow compatriots and artists. We visited castles and the caves at Pech Merle. We attended art gallery openings and concerts and a pottery festival.

Oh, and we shopped! And since I was on a budget, I also did a lot of simple window shopping or, as the French say, *le lèche-vitrines:* "we licked the window." As an American traveler, full of curiosity, I tried to deconstruct what the arrangement of the mannequins in a window might truly mean. I took thousands and thousands of photographs of ordinary things. I also drank a lot of wine. I ate a lot of cheese. Delicious yogurt. Hundreds of baguettes, with fresh butter from the farmers' market—oh dear, here I am confessing—again in true American style!

During all this, I asked Frenchwomen (and men) about their secrets to happiness. We talked about family, community, work, love, marriage, growing older, and body issues. We discussed their penchant for being fifteen minutes late, why Frenchwomen tend to be a little secretive at times, and what's the big deal with the five-hour dinner party. I've been invited to have tea in these women's gardens, to take a look and see what's in their refrigerators, to discuss their buying habits, how they handle money, their secrets to keeping their love lives interesting, and yes, I've even seen their under things—which by the way, are quite beautiful. We've talked about growing older, how to stay healthy and sexy at every age. And we've discussed the joys of a simple life, how pets can bring us comfort, the Frenchwoman's relationship with food, health, and fitness. Oh, and I've even attended their Weight Watchers meetings. Yes, they have Weight Watchers in France!

As Americans, we dress for success. We are always on the run and we grab our grande mocha lattes and drink them while driving. And we rush through our household chores with the help of the latest gadget. We want the newest car—whether it's the biggest SUV or the latest and greatest model in fuel efficiency. We approach every new trend with a kind of childlike zeal, bursting into the room with our arms extended, singing, "More, more, more!"

But at the end of the day, does all this rushing around, all this accumulating of *stuff* and jumping on board to grab the biggest, brightest, coolest, time-saving, convenient, new-new-new thing really bring us happiness? With all our success and expensive vacations, our big houses and bigger mortgages and our brand-new cars—have we become so satiated that we're really a little miserable, feeling a little let down by the pursuit of material goods? And have we forgotten how to find simple, old-fashioned, down-to-earth happiness?

AND THIS BRINGS ME back to my French grandmother and how she took hours to give me a shampoo and set, her fingers working the soap through my hair, slowly rinsing it with warm water, and toweling it dry, then sitting by me, wordlessly separating the strands and slowly removing the snarls with her fingers, one by one.

The beauty and meaning of this gift was brought back to me when Jessica Lee and I visited Besançon. We stayed with Marie Joëlle, a fashionable Frenchwoman who owns her own hair salon. Marie Joëlle spoke no English and at that time, my French was still quite rusty. Nonetheless, we were *sympathique* and we communicated with simple phrases and gestures. On the final day of our visit, Jessica and I were in the salon and Marie Joëlle said she wanted to shampoo my hair for me. At first, I was taken aback. I even felt that she was possibly being critical by offering this. Perhaps she thought my hair was really a mess and I was in desperate need of help! But no, she just wanted to give me this gift.

And so she did. She put a smock on me and had me sit in the salon chair, I leaned my head back in the sink while she leaned over me, working the warm water and then the fragrant shampoo into my hair.

Slowly but surely, I found myself crying. Tears streamed down my cheeks and ran down my neck and into the soapy water. I could not explain this to Marie Joëlle, but I knew that this was more than the gift of a shampoo. This was the gift of bringing my grandmother back to me, the experience of my childhood, recalling her accent, the softness of her voice, the perfumed smell of soap, the feeling of gentle hands on my scalp. The kindness of this simple and generous act.

I will tell you this now: I have lived a fairly comfortable life. I have been given many gifts in my life, but the gift of this shampoo was by far one of the most important gifts I've ever received.

And to me, this is the essence of French *joie de vivre.* It is a gesture. An experience. It is the fleeting moment in time that can never be repeated and must be appreciated now before it flies away, gone forever.

It's about being present and alive to the ordinary moment. It's about friendship and the knowledge that nothing lasts forever. It is Zen. And for the Frenchwoman, I believe, it is the heart of her happiness.

This book is my gift to American readers. My intention is to show you some simple ways you can keep your authentic American style, your enthusiasm and can-do spirit, and still incorporate some French *joie de vivre* into your life. It is also a love letter to the French; especially to Frenchwomen, and most especially, to my grandmother.

CHAPTER ONE

Joie de Vivre!

There is only one happiness in this life—to love and to be loved.

—GEORGE SAND

Looking for Happiness

IN AMERICA, WE ARE entitled to "life, liberty, and the *pursuit of happiness.*"

There is no such expression in France. In fact, in France, the equivalent expression is *la recherche du bonheur* (looking for happiness). On the surface, this might seem as if I am splitting hairs, but if you really examine the idea of "looking" for happiness as opposed to "pursuing" happiness, you'll see there's actually a big difference.

If we're looking for something, it feels as if it's there hiding in plain sight. It's under the table, for instance. And all we have to do is be patient and when the room is quiet, quickly lift up the tablecloth and *voilà!* There it is! Happiness!

On the other hand, pursuing implies a kind of chasing

after something. For us, happiness is down the street somewhere, but moving fast. We'll have to move even faster. We'll have to put on our cross trainers and chase after it, really chase it down, faster than the competition. Maybe we'll even have to push a few people to the side in our pursuit, until we final wrestle it to the ground and capture it.

Or perhaps we believe we already have happiness, but we're a little insecure in our lives and so we want to send out a message to the world. Perhaps we'll buy a big car and a bigger house to let everyone know, including ourselves that *"we're happy, dammit!"*

"Looking for happiness" seems gentler. There is happiness, and we just need to look. Perhaps happiness is sitting there in our garden and is nestled between the green leaves and the fragrant tomatoes. Then again, perhaps we just need to open a few cupboards and take out some nice spices and melt a bit of butter in a pan on the stove. Then again, perhaps happiness is in the eyes of our loved ones and we only need to look, to put on some music, take their hand, and dance. It's not something we can truly own. We certainly can't purchase it.

Isabelle is a thirty-six-year-old Frenchwoman living in Paris. She's traveled all over the world and she works in personal development. She's also incredibly articulate and wise beyond her years. I recently met her in Paris and we talked about life and love and family and work. Later, she wrote this about what *joie de vivre* means to her:

> *Joie de vivre* is about loving life, loving people, loving to be alive, feeling alive. It is about smiling, being in your heart, and being grateful for all the

> beautiful things in your life: being in good health, being able to hear, to see, to walk, being grateful for all the lovely and loving people (people we know or strangers we meet), being grateful for the nature surrounding us and all that it gives to us. It is to be grateful for the mystery of life, that we are able to live and breathe. . . . *Joie de vivre* is about sharing with others, smiling, laughing, making people feel a little less down, feeling useful to one another, making them believe in the future. It is making the choice to be positive.
>
> *Joie de vivre* is about trusting that nothing happens without a reason, and everything can turn out positive in the future. It is about accepting what's in your life in the moment and feeling contented inside.

This kind of happiness is already within you, and it's simply a matter of choosing to embrace the simple beauties of life. Perhaps happiness is right there with you at this very moment. In fact, he's upstairs taking a shower, getting ready for his day and whistling a catchy little tune. Yes, love is *joie de vivre.*

Laura K. Lawless is a dedicated Francophile behind the *Guide to Learn French* at About.com, a free website for students, teachers, and lovers of French. Laura is also the author of seven books, most recently *Intermediate French for Dummies.* She's lived in the South of France with her husband since 2008. This is what she tells me about *joie de vivre:*

> I think of *joie de vivre* as optimism about one's life and the ability to enjoy what you have without

> worrying too much about what you don't. Finding joy in the everyday isn't necessarily easy, but it helps a lot to share your life with someone you love. I was fortunate enough to meet my husband and partner, in every sense of the word, fifteen years ago, and together we have created a life of adventure, laughter, and joy, even when money, job stress, or the weather all seem to be conspiring to get us down. When we feel too poor to go out to movies and restaurants, we think up cheaper alternatives: we raid the recycling bin for art supplies, make each other scavenger hunts, seek out fancy recipes made from inexpensive food, and reminisce about great trips we've taken and meals we've eaten. We both recognize and appreciate how lucky we are to have each other, and our shared *joie de vivre.*

So you see, this kind of happiness has nothing to do with how much money you might have in the bank. However, it does have a lot to do with having a big heart and a strong imagination.

Dancing with the Stars

A few years ago I visited the small town of Gien with my husband. He was there to take part in a science conference not far from Cannes, and I was basically along for the ride. We stayed at a modest, family-style resort hotel. It was off-season, so the place was rather empty, except for about one hundred climate change scientists (who are a rugged bunch. I like to think of them as the Indiana Joneses of the science world) and a group of elderly French people. This was a funny combination—these rather serious international climate change scientists with a group of about fifty fun-loving French who often travel together. We met up with them at meal times and then later in the evening, but generally the two groups kept to themselves.

Then one night, while my husband was having a heated discussion on uranium series carbon dating with a couple of scientists from Great Britain, I heard the sounds of music and so I wandered off and found myself in the social room. There was a small but very lively band, including a singer playing the accordion. The Frenchwomen were dressed up in colorful, swirling skirts and everyone was dancing or standing or sitting near the dance floor, talking and laughing and having a great time. This was obviously the place to be. And so I decided to sit down and watch for a while. And then, suddenly, a rather chubby Frenchman sat right down on my lap! He began laughing and saying something very fast in French and I honestly couldn't understand him. Plus, he was bouncing up and down on my lap, which was very distracting. The ladies next to me did their best to explain what was happening, but they spoke no English and I was left even more confused, until I realized he was saying, *"Danse! Danse! Danse!"* And I tried in my terrible French (honestly, I'm better now!) to say, *"Mon mari n'est pas lá!"* (My husband is not here.) But still, he persisted. *"Danse, danse, danse!"* And then one of the ladies took my hand and said something about "*avec vous!"* And I understood that he wanted to dance with me and before I knew it, I was up there on the dance floor, going round and round, twirling breathlessly and laughing, and you know what? This chubby French guy was some heck of a great dancer. He was very strong and very sure of himself and he had loads of stamina. What fun! I gave myself over to the music and the movement and the arms of this very sweet man. The dizzying quality of being swung about the room, twirling and dipping, the closeness of the other dancers, the blur of faces and legs, shoes and smiles. My heart beating. And then breathing harder. Even sweating. The music built to a crescendo. All this brought me to a place of *rapture.* Well, if not that, then certainly happiness. Definitely *joie de vivre.* And when all was said and done, I had a really good time. Thanks to the funny French gentleman who sat on my lap.

Let the Good Times Roll

And actually, the word "happiness" translates as *bonheur* in French, which literally means a "good hour" or "good time." It's something you *experience.* You can't own a dance. You can't bottle a man and take him home with you and then take him out of the bottle when you need a good laugh and a pick-me-up. Inherent in the French concept of happiness is the knowledge that time is limited and joy is fleeting. It's a moment, never to be repeated. Dancing captures this feeling beautifully, because it involves all the senses—touch, sound, sight, smell, and even taste if the dance leads to a stolen kiss.

Dance can lift your mood and, yes, change your life. It's a fleeting joy, but honestly, the experience of dancing to good music is so much more powerful and lasting than something you might buy in a store and bring home with you.

Babette's Feast

When I asked Sylvie Gourlet, the artist and documentary filmmaker who lives in Paris, what she thought *joie de vivre* meant, she told me to rent the Danish film *Babette's Feast*. "This is a true example of *joie de vivre*." Without giving away too much, I will tell you this—the film's climactic moment evolves around the most lavish dinner party imaginable. Babette sacrifices everything to give this gift—this experience—of the most sensual, delicious, life-changing fête. No detail is spared when it comes to the preparation, the serving, and the partaking of the astoundingly sensual and delicious meal. And while the diners try to resist, ultimately they are transformed by the beauty, the generosity, and the unforgettable pleasure of Babette's feast. There is even a spiritual undertone to the film, as if to say good food, company, *joie de vivre* will save you. And I loved the message that if you are an artist, you will never be poor. And certainly Babette is *une véritable artiste de la cuisine*!

The next time you are tempted to microwave your dinner and eat all by yourself in front of the television, think about Babette. It's true, we lead busy lives and it's not always possible to create a sit-down dinner for one's entire family, but if you can plan a group dinner, even once a week, you'll see your life change.

And even when Frenchwomen microwave a dinner (yes, they do occasionally), they will take it out of the plastic container, put it on a nice plate, serve a salad beside it, and sit down at the dinner table with their family. Oh, and they'll really have a conversation. One conversation builds on another and another and before you know it, you are truly connected to your family and friends. And that's because there really is something to this idea of "breaking bread together."

My Red Leaf Lettuce Epiphany

I will make a confession. I tend to get a little panicky when I go to the supermarket. Perhaps it's the enormity of the place, or the people with the big shopping carts, the glaring lights, the hypnotic music telling me to buy, buy, buy! Then again, perhaps it's all the signs shouting at me that paper towels are on special, or to buy two for the price of one. It may be the overwhelming plentitude of choices: fifty different kinds of breakfast cereals and ten different brands of yogurt, each one with five different flavors.

When I was thirty-two, my husband and two-year-old daughter and I moved from New York City to Huntington Beach, California. Eventually, I would end up going to UCLA for a graduate school program in screenwriting, but I didn't know this at the time. At the time, I convinced my husband and myself that we would be happy if we just got out of the big city and raised our daughter in the country, by the sea.

Little did I know that we would end up in a land of unlimited choices: Orange County, California. Many people have suggested that unhappiness is not caused so much by lack, but by having so many choices it's impossible to focus in on what we really want and what we need. Because of this inability to focus, we get confused and we are no longer able to see clearly who we are and what we are supposed to be doing in this world. Hence, too many choices in yogurt will send me into an existential crisis.

And this brings me back to Huntington Beach, California. One day, I walked into the Pavilions—a gigantic supermarket. I walked up and down the aisles, my heart thumping, full of confusion. My face flushed, as I struggled with this overwhelming feeling that I could never be good enough, smart enough. I worried about my little daughter, my marriage, my writing career, and I wondered what the heck I was doing in this life. Here I was in the land of sunshine, and there was so much wealth around me, and everyone was saying how lucky I was to live in Huntington Beach, but the truth was we were kind of broke and I missed New York City and I feared I had made a terrible mistake. I missed the gritty streets, the small markets in Astoria, Queens (we had moved there from Greenwich Village for the last year before coming west). I missed working for Estée Lauder in the GM Building and coming home every night on the RR train and picking up the ingredients for dinner at the fish store, the green grocery, the little bakery. I had my own little French village in this mostly Greek and Italian neighborhood. But there was no grass or trees and no fresh air for my daughter, and the winters were miserable.

And so I found myself in Huntington Beach, a place that was so foreign to me, I might as well have been on Mars. And now I was in the supermarket faced with a plethora of choices, in a state of frenzy. I walked quickly, trying to figure out what it was I was supposed to buy in the first place. Then I remembered how my Weight Watchers leader told us to "walk the circumference of the supermarket," meaning avoid the aisles in the middle that held the most dangerous foods: the processed foods, the foods full of sugary and fatty goodness. She told us to stick to the outside—the dairy, meat, fish, and produce aisles. So I did.

And this is where I had my life-altering experience—what I like to call my Red Leaf Lettuce Epiphany. It was 1986 and I honestly had never seen red leaf lettuce before. I knew about iceberg lettuce, romaine, and butter lettuce (which my grandparents grew in Connecticut). But here in the Huntington Beach Pavilions produce aisle, there must have been twenty different kinds of lettuce. And they all looked so beautiful, so green, so vibrant and fat, arranged in such a way that they seemed to be bursting out of their displays and begging me to buy them. All of them! And I stood there, paralyzed. I couldn't decide. There were so many choices. And then, the automatic sprinkler system switched on and sprayed all the vegetables, drenching the lettuce in water. This was also something I had never seen before, so I just stared. After a minute, I found myself focusing on the bunches of red leaf lettuce. They were so pretty—the reddish-green leaves, and they made me think of a ruffled cancan girl's skirt bordered in ruby red and the sparkling dew from the supermarket produce water seemed like sequins sewn on a dress.

It was in this moment that I found illumination. Staring at the droplets of water on the leaves, I confess, I felt pure, unadulterated happiness. Those bunches of red leaf lettuce were so beautiful and so simple and, honestly, right there in the Huntington Beach supermarket, I began to cry. I cried big, fat tears of joy. And as corny as this may sound, I felt I learned something so valuable—and that was that I don't need a big cartful of stuff to make me happy. I don't need *things* in order to calm my nerves. Rather, happiness comes from slowing down and looking. Really looking. Happiness is not "out there." It's right in front of you. If you look, happiness is right there among the bunches of red leaf lettuce.

The Mysteries of Time

My French tutor, Marceline, grew up in Grenoble, France, during World War II. During a recent meeting, she told me how one of the first things she learned about America in her English class was the saying "time is money." This expression says so much about our culture. If time is money, then when we do something that does not involve getting paid, is it a waste of time? A waste of money? If this is true, then I suppose my Red Leaf Lettuce Epiphany was not worth much and, in fact, in this equation, the time I spent standing in the produce department actually cost me money. If time is money, then I suppose dinner parties and dancing and laughing with your friends is a waste of money. Playing with your children is nonproductive. Making love . . . well, you see where I'm going with this.

These things take little time and cost no money, or very little money, and are the things that bring us joy.

So where should we look for happiness?

Well, you can find happiness anywhere and everywhere. Truth be told, happiness is like the artist's muse. She is very whimsical and loves to play little tricks on us. If we search too hard, happiness will slip away. And then, when we are not really concentrating on capturing her, she will suddenly appear in our peripheral vision wearing a green silk gown, winking at us.

Happiness visits you when you're swimming in a pool and you notice how your pastel blue nail polish matches the water. Or she comes to you when you're standing in your kitchen chopping up tomatoes for ratatouille and your husband comes up behind you, takes you in his arms for a quick dance across the linoleum floor. Then again, she might perch on your shoulder one evening while you are sitting all alone in your parked car listening to an old Neil Young song. Happiness often comes in the most unlikely and unexpected situations, when we are not really looking for it. You are at your mother's funeral and suddenly your father—yes, your father, who has always been so stoic and quiet—gets up and sings the old Bob Hope tune "Thanks for the Memories."

In the middle of the tears, you find yourself laughing.

But, here's the difficulty—these moments are all very different and completely unique. Still, they are always available to you if you open the window to your heart. Sometimes, this simply means getting out in nature more. Walking on the beach. Then again, the muse of happiness might pop up indoors—in a church or a temple. She occasionally pals around with Bacchus, the god of wine—but not all the time. She's much too fickle for that. You might find yourself feeling very blue, as if nothing ever changes and your luck has run out, and so you hunker down and focus on what's in front of you. There is a task at hand, and you must let go of your grasping for success or money or love or whatever. The muse of happiness responds to this scenario, because you see, she's also a little like that frisky orange tabby cat you want to catch and hold. She runs away from you, but then you get busy and work and suddenly, feeling slightly ignored, she will appear out of nowhere and jump on your desk. Yes, doing simple ordinary work—even washing the dishes or raking leaves in the backyard—will coax the muse of happiness out of hiding.

But be on the lookout, because the form she takes will probably not be what you planned or expected. However, it will be perfectly right for you at that moment in time.

The truth is, she will appear wherever and whenever you are truly alive and present to the moment, when you stop to breathe, and to truly love this life.

Joie de vivre is an attitude. It's a decision you make to live a life of joy. It's an invitation to this dance called life. All you have to do is leave the door slightly ajar and listen for the music.

French Lessons

THE NEXT TIME you're out in the world, stop and focus. Try to be present to the simple joys you can find when doing everyday, ordinary tasks. Open your eyes to the possibilities for joy in simple and very familiar activities such as grocery shopping, gardening, cooking, sitting in a park, having a picnic, enjoying a bath, or even doing housework. Yes, even sweeping the kitchen floor can bring you *joie de vivre*, if you take your time and focus on the rhythm and motion of the broom, the whispering-whisking sound it makes and how this connects you with so many others before you who have swept a kitchen floor. And if you "dress the part," perhaps by wearing a kerchief around your hair, you can add a little more fun and whimsy to the experience.

Once and for all, break the connection between spending

money and happiness by finding experiences that bring you joy, but do not cost a thing. Take the time to feel your feelings and make a note to yourself when something very simple brings you great joy. Sources of joy are different for different people, so it's important that you register where your personal *joie de vivre* "lives." Make a list of the moments in your life in which you've felt most happy and consider this to be your "happiness personality profile."

Resist chasing after happiness and give happiness a chance to sneak up on you and "find" you in unexpected moments.

Next, find your "temple" of happiness. It might be out of doors, but this place where your happiness muse visits you might be in a dusty library or a crowded coffee shop. You can encourage the muse to visit you just by showing up on a regular basis.

Be creative with less. Enjoy the ordinary moments in a marriage or friendship or any relationship. Be playful. Be kind to yourself.

And finally, dance.

CHAPTER TWO

La Femme d'un Certain Âge

Age does not protect you from love. But love, to some extent, protects you from age.

—ANAÏS NIN

YOU SEE THEM all around Paris. The stylish and oh-so-elegant older woman. She's the one standing in front of you at the rue de Rivoli crosswalk. First, you notice her silhouette. There is something unmistakably sophisticated about her. Perhaps it's her posture. Her confident stance. From the back, you have no idea what her age might be. But you know, or should I say, you *sense* a certain worldliness. She's just too confident and contained to be *une jeune fille* (a young girl). There's something about her clothing—the sheer black stockings, the high heel pumps, the secret agent trench coat, and those big sunglasses, even though it's a gray day—but it's more than this. It's her attitude. She knows where she's going. And yet, she offers you a certain mystery. The promise of adventure. Perhaps she's planning a trip to Prague. Or she has a summerhouse in Deauville. Perhaps she has a lover there? Or a gentleman friend that she's just very fond of—no one really knows for sure.

She's just come from W.H. Smith. Yes, the English language bookstore. She likes to keep up her English language skills and she wants to read that new American novel in its original language. She is carrying a small tote and inside of it, you will find a lilac-colored box of *macarons* from the famous Ladurée. She is hosting a dinner party tonight and this little sweet will be part of the evening's celebration. Nothing fancy. Just elegant. Her daughter and son-in-law are coming home for the weekend and bringing the grandchildren. Her brother will be there, along with a colleague from Italy. And of course, our elegant *femme d'un certain âge* has invited her sister, the architect, who lives in Toulouse, but is visiting Paris for business.

So you can see, the party is quite a mixed bag, and intergenerational. This is one of the secrets of Frenchwomen. They don't just pal around with women their own age, but they enjoy the company of lots of different people—young, old, male, female, urban, rural, French, and non-French. And they enjoy being a mentor. They don't hide the fact that they've lived and learned and traveled and have had a wide range of experiences.

Our *femme* doesn't fuss over the dinner party. She's prepared a traditional French cassoulet (it was her mother's recipe) earlier in the day or the day before and since she's purchased the bread and the dessert, now it's just a matter of making a salad, putting out the cheese for the dessert course, and chilling the champagne and opening the wine.

Imagine her arriving home. She opens the door to the courtyard, her high heels making a pleasant clicking sound on the cobblestone, and then she quickly makes her way up the three flights of the winding circular staircase. If we were invisible and could observe her unnoticed, this is what we would see: she takes off her sunglasses, her scarf, her coat, and we see her face for the first time. Yes, our French *femme d'un certain âge* is what we would call "middle-aged." But she is so much more than this. Yes, there are crinkles around her eyes. Obviously, she's laughed and cried many times in her life. Oh, and there's the slight parenthesis lines framing her mouth. All those smiles. Thousands of them. Her hair might be colored a rich chestnut and then again, it might be artfully streaked with silver. If our *femme* is from the Left Bank and owns a gallery, she may have colored her hair a shocking shade of red. She wears a classic black dress, but it is adorned with the most exquisite jewelry—each piece holds a memory, an experience. There is the big silver bangle from her trip last year to Morocco. There's the pearl necklace her husband gave her on their fifth wedding anniversary. She wears an unusual brooch that belonged to her grandmother. Perhaps this is her "signature" piece. Then again, her trademark might be her fabulous legs that she likes to show off by wearing slightly expensive textured stockings. She knows this is one of her best features, so why not show them off in the best light?

Her apartment? It's filled with fresh flowers and original art. Not necessarily expensive art—but beautiful and occasionally quirky pieces created by family and friends or from a favorite artist that she's been collecting for years.

That's really the key to the *femme d'un certain âge*. History and experience. She's not afraid to show you that she's lived. Really lived. She's traveled. She's known many, many people. She's lived a full life and continues to do so. She doesn't dress like she's twenty, because well, why would she want to? Why would she want to dress or act as if she does not possess all that knowledge and experience the world has given her? She's proud of the fact that she has lived—truly lived—that she's seen so much and that her life continues to unfold before her in a most interesting way. And more than this—she's lived long enough to know how to handle life's little and not-so-little upsets. These days, there's not much that unravels her. She knows who she is. She knows her powers, her gifts, her limitations, and her weaknesses. She knows how to take in stride life's little disappointments, as well as the bigger demands of being a grown-up in this world.

And you know what? All this makes our *femme d'un certain âge* very, very sexy. What she gives up in terms of a youthful, dewy-eyed innocence, she gains in elegance, style, sophistication, and wisdom.

I talked with one gorgeous *femme d'un certain âge* who lives in Paris. Her name is Micheline Tanguy and she owns her own company as a personal and professional image consultant. She's an expert in style, body image, and how to communicate confidence. When I asked her to tell me what is the Frenchwoman's secret to beauty and elegance, she said it's not simply one thing. Rather, it's a totality of things, such as how she stands up, how she walks, the way she holds her handbag. She told me:

> It means being attractive for yourself. We do our best to reach this aim in our daily life. I must confess, it's not only about appearance. It's also about self-esteem, self-confidence, respect, and love for ourselves. It's about knowing what we want . . . and self-respect.

Yes, self-respect.

Go, Cougars!

The truth is, no matter where you live—even in France—it's not easy getting older, but this is especially true for women in America. All around us, we are bombarded with daily images of beautiful young women—or should I say girls. These young, long-legged, smooth-skinned creatures grace the pages of our fashion magazines, star in our movies, and even have their own reality television shows—as if we really care whether *Pretty Wild Girls* are going to get arrested this weekend. True, occasionally, you will see a Helen Mirren or a Meryl Streep or a Susan Sarandon at the Oscars and everyone will *ooh* and *aahh*, pronouncing how fabulous they are and how gorgeous they look . . . *for their age*! But these beautiful women are the exception and not the rule. And so, if you are a woman of a certain age, it's easy to grow discouraged and begin to believe that unless you have been anointed as "the beautiful older woman of the year"—the singular example that we are not an ageist society—it's easy to just give up.

On the other hand, we now have "cougars." Yes, predatory older women who wear a lot of leopard print and supposedly go after younger men. You will seldom find an older woman who describes herself as a cougar unless she's making a little joke. Rather, it's the young men who are looking for hot, older women who have come up with this term. (Although, we should note that a recent French survey found that fully 90 percent of women over fifty in France say they are sexually active.)

You see the problem here: We are being defined by someone else—the media, or men on the prowl, or someone who wants to sell you something. Wrinkle cream, perhaps? Or maybe we're being sold something a little more nefarious. Perhaps we're being sold the idea that it's okay to be an older woman, as long as your main interest is still finding and pleasing a man.

With all these messages coming at us every day, it's difficult to really see ourselves, as we really are right now. No, you may not be young, but you're not *finished* yet, either. In fact, I would like to propose that you are actually just beginning.

This is because, as we grow older, our true selves emerge. But more than this, what we might lose in youth, we gain in confidence. Not the false bravado of a wild twenty-something, but the true power of a woman who has lived and learned. That's the power of Helen Mirren, Meryl Streep, Susan Sarandon, and our famous French *femmes*—Juliette Binoche, Catherine Deneuve, and Isabelle Adjani.

How to Save Your Life

Last fall in the town of Valence d'Agen, I followed a gorgeous older woman walking around the farmers' marketplace. She was wearing high heels and carrying a wicker basket for her purchases. No, she wasn't a "cougar." She certainly was not trying to act younger than she really was. In fact, rather than denying her age, she seemed to be reveling in the benefits of being *une femme d'un certain âge.* This particular woman was wearing a pair of interesting eyeglasses and some artful jewelry. Oh, and of course, she was wearing a scarf. It was very colorful and loosely draped around her shoulders. I loved watching her walk from market stall to market stall. I stood for a moment to witness how she picked up one perfectly ripe red tomato, held it for a moment in the palm of her hand as if weighing it, and then brought it up to her nose and inhaled deeply. After this, she chatted with the farmer for several minutes, laughed over some shared story, and then, with the help of this farmer and friend, made her selections. She clearly had been going to this marketplace for years and had established a wonderful rapport with the shopkeepers. She was sexy and intriguing—not so much because of her good looks, but because of her savoir faire, her confidence and self-assurance.

That's really the key. Once you get to a certain point in your life, a lot of the old insecurities fade away. And if you had children along the way, they are now grown. A whole new life opens before you and new possibilities present themselves to you. Some dreams that you deferred now resurface. There's actually a term for this in astrology (I learned this from thc wonderful astrologist Susan Miller). It's called your "Saturn return," which means that the lessons and challenges and decisions you made during your late twenties revisit you in your forties up to about age fifty-nine. At this stage, you have another opportunity to reconsider the past and change the course of your life. If there are leftover dreams from those early years, you can now embrace them again and bring them to fruition. It's actually a very magical and powerful time in any person's life. So, rather than thinking of this phase as a "midlife crisis," consider that this is actually another chance to grab the brass ring. True, you may not be as agile or quick as you were in your twenties, but now you have all that wisdom and power and experience. Oh, and by now you know how to admit you don't know how to do something and you're not too proud to ask for help. And most importantly, you've learned not to pay attention to the naysayers and you've let go of the debilitating desire for perfection.

This was the case for my good friend Marjorie, a sound artist and university professor. She's been living in the north of France for the last twenty years. She was born in Michigan, moved to New York City after attending the University of Michigan, and spent nearly twenty years in New York, first as an actress, then a writer, and she wrote and produced a Peabody Award-winning radio documentary drama, establishing a lifetime career in public radio. She is one talented and accomplished *femme d'un certain âge*, but with all that said, she's now taken up singing American jazz classics with an ensemble.

She tells me that the French love American jazz and are very accepting of less than completely polished voices. In fact, Marjorie tells me that they actually prefer *personality* over *perfection*. It's the passion and authenticity that stirs them!

Marjorie recently told me this:

> When I was young I desperately wanted to be an actress and I also loved to sing and dance. I was totally obsessed with this idea from the age of twelve, when my mother sent me to drama class to give me confidence, to the age of around twenty-seven, when I finally gave it all up and got a real job.
>
> The little girl that sang all the words to "I'm the Greatest Star" over and over again in her bedroom suffered quite a number of indignities in early adulthood. Two years of rejection on the stand-up

comedy circuit, as well as a complete lack of encouragement during the short period that I sang alone with a piano player in a small showcase bar where I also worked as a waitress.

Childhood piano lessons came to nothing. I bought a guitar in my twenties and never even learned to tune it properly. Still, I listened to jazz by the hour and learned hundreds of songs in my head. As an apprentice in summer stock, I couldn't even clap in rhythm. However, in the summer of 1972, there was a big flood in the town, and they sent all the professional actors home and the apprentices had to play all the leads, so I got onstage. But still, the word on me was that I couldn't really carry a tune.

In a way I kind of outgrew my performing complex and turned my ambitions in other directions. I turned to radio producing and eventually radio wasn't really artistically challenging enough, so I became more and more compositional in my work. But there was no real place for sound composers who weren't considered bona fide musicians first and foremost.

I cut everything in my life and moved to France, vaguely chasing a quiet place to become an artist—that certainly did not happen overnight. Another eighteen years went by.

I never stopped singing in my head. By chance, I was teaching in an engineering school with quite a number of conservatory musicians doing double majors—and somehow I got up the courage to perform in their concert at school. I was very apologetic and deprecating about it, but I think because they liked their crazy American teacher I was a hit.

The school celebrated its fiftieth anniversary and I was asked to help produce a show. We had a big theater with a professional sound system, a student who was a piano prodigy as the music director, and a full band. The show was packed to the rafters. At the end of the show, the band had wanted to play "Everybody Needs Somebody to Love" à la the Blues Brothers, so I came out dressed like John Belushi—sunglasses, pork pie hat—and did the song, monologue and all. My team of students came out, all dressed as the Blues Brothers and backed me up in a line dance.

Right before we went on, the one female engineer in the team whispered, "Are you nervous?" I said, "Not really." She said, "You're not? Why?" "I dunno. There just doesn't seem to be any point to being nervous. I'm gonna go out there and do it, that's all."

After the song, the place exploded into a standing ovation, and it was only later that I realized that this packed audience of about three hundred people were in fact mostly the guys that I had been entertaining and encouraging in English class for the last ten years and their spouses and families. The next day, a Saturday morning, I just sat and sobbed for about two hours, totally overwhelmed by this love and adoration.

So that led to singing in more concerts, performing with a group in a local restaurant, taking a three-day jazz master class that was horribly snobby and intimidating—and doing two art performances this month in which I sang. The last concert I did with the students was in February—I scatted to "Take Five," something I would never have been able to do even a year ago. That concert was the last time I rehearsed and performed without putting myself down and apologizing to the musicians.

They say that proper singing is about your breathing and how you stand, et cetera—that is all true—but I am sure that I was always capable of singing and performing—and that I had a good, ear, too—it was always there. I was just too scared. Even when I was throwing myself at an audience and trying my very best I was still too scared.

I'll be fifty-nine on my next birthday. I don't know what took me so long. I don't bother with regrets. It just took as long as it took.

Brain Power

In her latest book, *The Secret Life of the Grown-up Brain,* scientist Barbara Strauch explains how our brains actually get better in middle age. While some quick reflexes might diminish, our reasoning gets better, we're able to make better decisions, and our ability to quickly and accurately size up situations improves. Years ago, we heard that we lose 30 percent of our brain cells as we age and now we find that this is simply not true. Yes, just as we always suspected, we get better with age. But here's the catch—if you don't use it, you lose it, so she recommends challenging our minds. I'm happy to report that learning a foreign language is on her list of ways to build brain power, as well as getting into a conversation with someone who disagrees with your ideas. All this tones the brain. And it's very French! When we asked Frenchwomen and men how they stayed so vibrant and happy, they often cited how they took workshops and classes. My French friend Tania is already a terrific cook, but recently she took a class in making the French *macaron,* which apparently is a very delicate operation and not easy to master. She speaks perfect English and sometimes it's a struggle to get her to speak French, because she wants to practice her English! Recently, for her vacation, rather than just going to the beach or over the channel to London, she went to Egypt. You see the pattern here—she is always challenging herself. The French believe in always learning something new.

So, the next time you read about classes and workshops at your local community college or night school, sign up for something that challenges you. Your brain will thank you.

The Beautiful Alberta Hunter

In 1978, I was living in New York City and I learned that the famous jazz singer Alberta Hunter had come out of retirement and was going to sing at the Cookery in Greenwich Village. I immediately ordered tickets. I knew this would be a once-in-a-lifetime experience. Alberta Hunter, who had started her singing career back in the 1920s singing with Louie Armstrong, had stopped singing many years before to become a nurse, but was now retired. And at age eighty-something, the Cookery convinced her to come and sing. What a joy and a privilege to see this beautiful woman. And she was truly beautiful—not for an eighty-year-old woman, but beautiful for any age. And I loved the stories she told and all the songs she sang. But most of all, I remember Alberta Hunter singing the very, very randy song, "My Man Is Such a Handy Man." The entire song is made up of double entendres such as "he threads my needle. He creams my wheat." Her performance was brilliant—down to earth, funny, relaxed, wise, and very, very sexy.

Alberta Hunter was sexy—not despite the fact that she was eighty, but *because* of it. The fact that she was eighty-something added a complexity to the evening. She owned her sexuality, her worldliness. You felt as if she'd had some amazing love in her life and that she had a confidence and a sense of humor about it. And her age added a certain richness to the song. This was a woman who had lived and loved. Who had known fame and left it all behind to live an ordinary life and then was back again.

I will admit, too, that because of her age, I knew that she would not be long in this world and that I was experiencing an event never to be repeated. And indeed, Alberta Hunter died seven years later.

I tell you this story not simply to say that you are always becoming and the story is always unfolding, but as a message to be alive to the present moment and to know that while you may not be a famous jazz singer or a not-quite-famous jazz singer like my friend Margie, nonetheless—whether you know it or not—you are still being observed. You are still an inspiration to the young and the not-so-young. Every day, you have an opportunity to send out the message that aging isn't such a bad thing and it's certainly nothing to be afraid of. In fact, it's something quite delightful.

The Young and the Restless

If we deny our age and fight it, we are silently telling our daughters and younger people that aging is horrible. A nightmare! We are giving out the message that they should not grow old at any cost. And so, even twenty-five-year-olds begin to fear aging and want to rush to the plastic surgeon. This is a losing battle. Why not show the younger generation that becoming *une femme d'un certain âge* has many benefits and that aging can be wonderful and something to actually look forward to?

Borrow a page from the French. Frenchwomen do not take anything for granted. They've been through hell and back through centuries of invasions and wars and economic tumult. They have lost many of their young men to wars and so as Frenchwomen, they have learned to survive on their own. This loss is part of their secret to being a self-assured *femme d'un certain âge.* They appreciate what they have in their lives, no matter how much or how little.

And if you are reading this and you are in your twenties or thirties or forties, let me play *le rôle de votre mère* (the role of your mother) for a moment. I have been where you are—there is not enough money or time. The job is not rewarding or stimulating enough. The baby has a cold and is always sniffling. You're worried about your parents getting older. The house is a mess. Your husband seems to be preoccupied with work or your boyfriend broke up with you and now you are alone with this feeling you must begin all over again.

Here's the truth of life—you are always beginning all over again. Every day brings something new. Embrace it. One day you will look back at your life and realize you were a part of something grand! Something important. You are part of this moment in history.

As *une femme d'un certain âge*, I often hear people talk about the 1960s and the political unrest and turmoil, the hard-won sexual freedom. I stop and think—Wow, I lived through all that. I *remember* that. But honestly, at the time, I was often distracted by whether I was going to get my biology homework done in time or not. I seldom looked up from my own personal concerns to see the bigger picture and to find the balance of myself as an individual in the context of the larger world.

In the 1980s, when Mrs. Estée Lauder was still around, I worked in the international division and wrote fashion copy for the famous cosmetic company. I wrote about the prêt-a-porter for the spring and fall color stories. Oh, and I was around for the naming of the famous fragrance Beautiful. Now, that was a dramatic time!

I loved my job, but at the time I didn't think of it as more than a job. I spent most of my time wishing I could write for Hollywood! But at Estée Lauder, there were so many stories and once-in-a-lifetime experiences right there in front of me, I was completely nearsighted. Nowadays, people often tell me how glamorous it sounds and I have to take a step back and think—Yes, the truth is, in hindsight, the whole damn thing—this life, in fact—is glamorous!

So, appreciate what you have in this moment in your life and be present to the unfolding story right before you.

Your Unique Signature

When I first met Micheline Tanguy in Paris, she looked at me, eyes full of passion, and told me, "You want to know the secret of Frenchwomen and why she has confidence? *Ooh la la?*" And then she paused for effect and told me: "You are Woman. Just be!"

Sounds a bit like a Zen koan, doesn't it? But it's true. The world is a tumultuous, ever-changing place. But you must find a way to be still, to quiet the mind, whether it's through meditation or long walks or yoga or your Secret Garden (that real or metaphorical place that brings you peace and replenishment). As you age and as the world rumbles and roars into wild new directions, you must hold on to the things that make you *you.* And here, I'd like to suggest something radical to you, or perhaps just a little odd, but I suggest you practice your handwriting. Your handwriting, especially your signature, is something that is so personal and so revealing about who you are in this world. However, it's easy to get sloppy and forget all about those early days when we first learned to sign our names or write a love letter or how we carefully added our signatures to the very first check we wrote. I suggest that you practice the lost art of writing real letters and that you take your time to write neatly and to sign your name with a bit of panache, not because it's nice to do (though it *is* nice to do and in this age of e-mailing, it's also very impressive), but because this act of holding pen to paper and transferring the thoughts from your heart to your hand and down to your fingers and on to the page is a lesson in Zen. And it's a lesson in reconnecting to that little girl who first learned to write her name, and yes, to your truest, core self.

Plus, to write neatly and carefully is simply to be polite.

This act of focusing your attention on the little things that make you unique also applies to your voice. When you were a child, you discovered that a certain tone or pitch or volume would achieve certain results. But as we age, we take this very powerful and very individual part of our personality for granted and just as we might let our handwriting get a bit compromised, so, too, we can let our speaking voices deteriorate. Your voice is an instrument. It is powerful, seductive, intriguing, and completely unique. Why not bring some awareness to your voice. It's just as much a "signature" to your individuality as a real signature.

Find Your Balance

This will help you to visualize your truest self. Once you do this, you can let go of the things that do not belong in your life—both literally (clear out those closets and give away the things you no longer treasure) and figuratively (do you really need to still play the ingenue?). Once you let go, you open up space for new things, true things. For me, it was rediscovering my grandmother and reconnecting with the long-held but hidden dream of visiting France and finally mastering the language and understanding my roots. Let go of all your assumptions. Quiet your mind. Now, ask yourself, who are you truly? Who are you meant to be?

It's Never Too Late

I grew up in an era where there were no women of color on the covers of our fashion magazines. It was as if the whole world was white and African American or Latina women just didn't exist. I will never forget the day in 1974 when I picked up a copy of *Vogue* magazine. Right there, on the cover, was Beverly Johnson! A black woman! This was a first. I was in college by this time. It was an era filled with so many changes. There was the civil rights movement, and protests against the Vietnam War, the sexual revolution, and the women's movement—but to be honest, the day Beverly Johnson appeared on the cover of *Vogue* felt so important to me. I looked into her eyes and felt as if she was speaking directly to me, proclaiming the magical mutuality of what we think of as beauty. Her face announced to the world that it was time to shed our assumptions. And on a personal level, even though I was just a white girl from the suburbs, I felt as if she was saying to me, "And oh yeah, you're beautiful, too."

And now, we have Naomi Campbell and Tyra Banks and many, many other gorgeous and inspirational women. We do not question whether they are beautiful or not. We simply know.

This is how change happens. It takes someone to be brave, a little muscle, definitely a sense of imagination and then . . . *poof!* The world has changed and it feels as if it happened overnight. This one shift creates a magical ripple effect. And soon we forget the past and we can hardly remember the past, when things were not always so fair. We forget how narrow-minded we were. And we all say—well, yes, of course. Women—*in all their many incarnations*—are beautiful.

So, do something brave today. Go out in your town and be that beautiful older woman. Yes, be the message. And who knows, perhaps one day we will see *une femme d'un certain âge* on the cover of American *Vogue*!

French Lessons

RECONSIDER WHAT you wanted to do when you were in your twenties. Is there something you "put on the shelf" due to the demands of work and family? Could you possibly now revive and realize some of those old dreams in whole or in part?

Go through your belongings and give things away to younger friends. Share the wealth and leave room in your life for something new.

Once you've cleared out the clutter in your life, look around at what is left, what you could not possibly live without. Within this, you'll find your trademark, your signature. Perhaps it's a brooch that once belonged to your grandmother. Take it out of the jewelry box and wear it daily. Is it your collection of elegant beaded evening bags? Don't wait for that very special occasion, but rather bring them out into the daylight. Do you adore bright red lipstick? Even though red lipstick may be out of vogue and you've been told to retire it past a certain age, go ahead and indulge. In all this effort to be French and elegant, don't forget something the fabulous fashion doyenne Diana Vreeland once said: "Never fear vulgar, just boring. We all need a splash of bad taste; no taste is what I am against."

Your signature is literal and figurative. Take good care of both. I recommend that you take care of your handwriting. Frenchwomen always have beautiful handwriting. Take a lesson from the French and take your time when writing a check or a note. You'll find that this little adjustment will have a ripple effect through your entire life. By controlling your penmanship, you'll find it's easier to control any other sort of sloppiness that may have muscled its way into your life. The same goes for your speaking voice, your e-mails, your manners. A little self-awareness can go a long way.

Tend to the gifts nature has given you—your lustrous hair or your good figure. Indulge in spa days more often. Find moments to be still and reflect. After paring down what is no longer necessary in your life, update your look so that you are making the most of your best assets. If you've got great gams, then buy a pair of textured stockings and wear those with boots. If you wear eyeglasses, consider buying more artful frames. Be proud of your age and how your life experience makes you interesting to others. And sexy!

Challenge yourself and break out of the familiar. Travel. Learn a new language. Consider taking a class or teaching a class at your local community college.

Get intergenerational and avoid just mingling with people your own age. Become a role model to younger women. Be a mentor. Inspire someone every day by just being your own true self.

Appreciate the mystery that is here now. The wonderful thing about being *une femme d'un certain âge* is that people look up to you and want to hear what you have to say, because of your age, not despite it. Enjoy having come this far and knowing a thing or two.

CHAPTER THREE

Le Jardin Secret: The Secret Garden

Pour vivre heureux, vivons cachés.
(To live happily, live hidden.)

—FRENCH PROVERB

FRANCE IS A MYSTERIOUS COUNTRY. Oftentimes, at first glance she is closed to you. This is especially true in the countryside where there are fewer tourists and most especially true if you happen to arrive in the middle of the day. It's easy to imagine that she is not welcoming you and that indeed, you would have to stay for a long, long time and work very hard before she would open herself up to you.

If you are patient, and make a little effort, you will find that these stone walls will open to reveal beautiful courtyards, gardens, olive trees, flowers bursting into bloom—and the Frenchwoman herself, greeting you, well-rested and happy to receive you.

France is a woman. Here in America, we have Uncle Sam. But France is known as a woman—La Belle France. It's true we have the Statue of Liberty, holding up her torch to welcome the world, but then, she was a gift to us from the French.

My Lessons Begin

Last September, I took the overnight flight from Boston to Charles de Gaulle Airport. My French friend Tania had given me detailed instructions on how to get to her office on rue Cambon (the same street where Coco Chanel once lived). From there, I was to pick up the keys to her apartment, where I would drop off my luggage. In my dazed state, I could not find the bus and so I got on the RER train and took that to Gare du Nord.

This was not in the original directions. So, once I got off the train, I was completely confused, bleary-eyed and exhausted from the overnight trip. I had no idea what Métro I should take to get to L'Opéra and so I ended up in a taxi line and took a taxi, grateful to put down my luggage. I arrived at her office around ten in the morning, sweating a bit, feeling less than fresh, and completely out of sorts. I sat on one of the sleek white leather chairs in the elegant lobby and waited for Tania, as slender and stylish Frenchwomen came and went. And then finally, Tania came down the stairs to greet me. Her hair was pulled back in a neat little chignon and she was wearing a navy blue pencil skirt, a simple white shirt, and a colorful scarf tied around her neck. The quintessential Frenchwoman! She sat next to me, and I suddenly felt like a tortoise—very large, very slow, and very ancient.

It's true, I'm probably old enough to be her mother, but at that moment, I felt more like her grandmother. I immediately confessed that I had taken a taxi and she looked at me a little disapprovingly (or perhaps that was my imagination) and proceeded to give me directions to her apartment in the Fourteenth Arrondissement, which involved more walking, more Métros and another bus, and absolutely no taxis.

The Secret Behind the Door

This time, I made myself follow her directions to the letter and I resisted the desire to fling my luggage and myself into the nearest taxi. Truthfully, I felt rather pleased, when I was able to negotiate changing Métros and finding the bus and getting off at the right stop. All was well with the world or so I thought as I stood in front of the enormous, ornate door and took out Tania's key.

But then, the key didn't work! I kept trying and trying and honestly I felt like sitting on the curb and crying. I was so close to a hot shower and a comfy bed and yet so far away. Finally, I asked a passing lady with a baby stroller if she could help me with *la clé*, because I imagined there must be some French secret to this key that I was not getting. And indeed, this was absolutely the case. The French lady explained to me that I simply needed to press a certain button. I did, and *voilà*, the big door opened easily to reveal a lovely cobblestoned courtyard. I walked in and found the door to which the key magically (actually quite obviously) fit. From there, I walked up the circular, winding staircase to the third floor (which was called the fourth floor, but that's because the ground floor doesn't count—that's called the *rez-de-chaussée* and the first floor, which we would call the second floor is called the *premier étage*). You could see why I was in a state of confusion! Pulling my luggage up the stairs with me, I went up and around and up and around and up and around until I felt the dizzying effect of knowing that I was far, far from home and all that was familiar.

Later in my journeys I would come to realize that this circuitous route—the Métro, the bus, the walking, the secret courtyards, and the winding stairs—were all essential ingredients to French mystery and confidence.

A Long and Winding Road

And even then, in the midst of my exhaustion and confusion, I couldn't help but think that years and years of walking up and down these stairs—something amazing must happen to the brain. A new pathway must form and it must change the Frenchwoman's approach to life. Certainly, the stairs immediately force one to stand up straight and focus, not hurry, but to be present to the moment. And of course, these stairs are mighty theatrical. Just imagine your husband or lover waiting for you at the bottom of these winding, curving, ornate stairs. And there you are—descending the steps, seen from below in glimpses, flashes of leg and heels as you walk down and around, mysteriously coming in and out of view, disappearing, then reappearing, until finally you emerge. By the time you reach that bottom step, I would think this man would be in a state of enchantment.

No wonder it's so easy for the French to reject the fast and efficient (an elevator, for instance) in favor of something that takes a little more time and delays gratification, but is ultimately much more satisfying. Deep in her cerebral cortex, the part that hides the mysteries of language and memory, a Frenchwoman holds the image of her first walk down those stairs, going round and round with her mother as she teaches her to sing "Au Clair de la Lune." These stairs must hold so many memories and secrets for the French, but more than this, the difficulty of negotiating these stairs makes one more conscious of posture, breathing, and presentation. No, they're not easy or quick or even sensible, but oh, they're lovely to look at and they make the simple act of descending the stairs an opportunity for drama and beauty.

But at this moment in time, I did not appreciate all this beauty. Instead, I braced myself and I walked up and around and up and around, huffing and puffing, cursing myself for being thoroughly out of shape. And finally, I entered Tania's apartment, looked around quickly, taking in the fact that her kitchen was small and modern, and her living room was dominated by a big round table with a big vase of fresh flowers on top of it. The sitting area was upstaged by this table and I imagined this is where she hosted her dinner parties. And that most of the interactions took place around this table. Yes, this was the place where romances blossomed and friendships were solidified—all within the context of delicious food and wine and laughter and talk.

Upstairs, there was a lovely bedroom and a bathroom, a guest bedroom, which was very inviting to my jet-lagged self.

Nonetheless, once I put my bags down and drank a glass of water, I did go back outside to the little *boulangerie* I had spied on the corner and I went in and ordered a baguette sandwich with fresh chicken and lots of vegetables. I confess, I returned and stood in Tania's little kitchen and I wolfed it down in a matter of seconds (not very French!). And then I took a shower. I did not take a bath in the enormous claw-foot bathtub, even though it was so beautiful and so enticing.

After the shower, I got into bed and immediately fell into a deep sleep, only to awake with a feeling of panic. I knew I would now have to get dressed and find my way back to Tania's office. I would have to walk or take a bus to the Métro, change Métros, then walk some more. And so, armed with my French-English dictionary, the Métro map, Tania's directions, and a great deal of determination, I managed. I actually arrived at Métro L'Opera a little early and had time to walk around and take photographs at the Chanel store and then stare at the delicate, multicolored *macarons* in the windows of the famous Ladurée.

And then, I sat in the lobby on the white leather chair and observed French office workers coming down the stairs and out the door. I saw no elevators. Instead, everyone seemed to come down these beautifully ornate stairs. And for me, sitting in the lobby, full of wonder—it was as if I was watching a fashion show! The men wore dark suits, white shirts, and brightly colored ties. Clearly, there was no such thing as casual Friday. The Frenchwomen wore stylish black dresses, scarves, fitted skirts in charcoal, black, and navy, and yes, I saw the occasional pair of jeans, but they were fitted perfectly to the woman wearing them and accompanied by an elegant white shirt and some baubles or bijoux. It seemed to me that they wore very few prints, but rather a basic palette of black, navy, and white or beige with a dash of color from a scarf or an interesting accessory—a trendy bag (or *sac*, as they call them) and some fabulous heels or cute ballet flats.

Finally, Tania arrived. She said that before we went to dinner, she wanted to pick up some tickets for an upcoming concert. Did I mind walking a bit more? "Oh, no, not at all!," I said. And we were off. Walking fast. And this was no short walk. By the time we had dinner and took the Métro and then the bus back to her apartment, I was ready to go directly to sleep.

But before I did, I noticed that Tania turned on her computer and checked e-mail for about fifteen minutes. She did not turn on the television. And unlike me—when confronted with my laptop and my e-mail—she did not spend hours at it. But rather, it seemed that her priority that evening was to enjoy a long, leisurely bath in that big, beautiful bathtub.

I was impressed by how self-contained she was and how she seemed to not share as much as my American girlfriends. And this is not just the case with Tania. I have encountered so many Frenchwomen and they simply don't "dish" the way Americans do. You know what I'm talking about—how we can meet a woman at a party and within five minutes we are sharing the most intimate details of our lives, our childhood, how we are having marital difficulties or we are feuding with our sister or how our oldest son is failing in school. The French just don't do this. They keep it hidden. Or at least they wait a long time before revealing all. This is part of their Secret Garden. And it is definitely part of how they keep their mystery and their confidence, because they never get that feeling that bits and pieces of their soul are scattered all about town.

Get Some Rest

Everyone knows that stress is bad for us. Stress makes us cranky and tired. We're more likely to make mistakes and to make decisions that we regret. Stress makes us unhealthy. It can lead to weight gain. It can lead to heart attacks. But you can reduce a lot of the stress in your life by simply creating a Secret Garden. This Secret Garden can be in your bedroom, where you spend a few hours every weekend, sleeping late, or reading in bed, writing in a journal or just daydreaming. Perhaps you don't have a house with pretty blue shutters, but you can block out the day's hustle and bustle and demanding light with a pretty silk sleep mask and a pair of earplugs. I know from personal experience that some lavender potpourri or scented candles can be incredibly soothing.

Your Secret Garden might also involve a long, luxurious bath with lavender oil. Then again, there are secret gardens that are real gardens. The French are brilliant at creating these sacred spaces—intimate and enchanting gardens behind stone walls. From the outside on the street, there is only a stone wall, but once you enter a gate, an entire world of lilacs and gardenias, tulips and roses, fruit trees and olive trees might be revealed. Your Secret Garden might be a small vegetable garden that you plant in the springtime and then tend to in the early morning and later afternoons. It could be a small herbal garden you keep on your deck or windowsill. Watching a garden grow—even in the city where your little garden might be part of a larger communal garden—is truly a Zen experience. When you first plant your lettuce, days go by and it seems as if nothing is happening. Your garden is not growing, but then one day—*voilà*! There are little green shoots coming up and if you did not know it, you might think they are only bits of grass or weeds, but with patience and time and water and sunshine, your garden grows.

Here's what my friend Marjorie tells me about the Secret Garden:

> In the French culture, it is frowned upon to be too forthcoming about yourself: your personal story, biographical details, opinions, the basic state of the inside of your mind at every minute. There's an expression that is often heard, *"Ne me raconte pas ta vie,"* or *"D'accord, j'arrête de raconter ma vie maintenant,"* which is like saying, "So, enough about me!" and meaning it.
>
> Now, I am still the kind of person that will reel off my entire life's story to a stranger in a ladies' room. Or am I? I correct that: I think I am much less that way, because while I have come to value my American sense of transparency, my American spirit of "continual improvement," the shark moving forward, I think I have also become more discreet, slightly less out there, perhaps even preserving a little mystery. A little.

The Town Where All the People Have Disappeared

I arrived in Auvillar, where my fellowship was to begin. Auvillar is in the Southwest, north of Toulouse and south of Bourdeaux. The Virginia Center for the Creative Arts Auvillar residency is in the Moulin à Nef, meaning the port area of the village, right by La Garonne River. Auvillar is officially one of France's "most beautiful villages." At the Moulin à Nef, there are fig trees, roosters crowing all day long, olive trees, oak forests, and vineyards. The center of the town has a magnificent eleventh-century cathedral and is built high up on a hill and surrounded by ancient stone walls that were designed to fend off foreign invasions.

After settling into my room and my studio, I decided I would walk into the village to buy a baguette and introduce myself to the local librarian. With great expectation, I walked up a very steep hill to get to the village from the Moulin à Nef. On the way, I passed a little *salon de thé* (tea salon) with a blackboard sign in the front where the pilgrims on their way to Compestella in northern Spain to pay homage to St. Jacques would find words of encouragement in French from fellow travelers. Finally, a bit breathless from the climb, I arrived in town. It was only a five-minute walk, but steep!

As I walked into the village, I found lovely cobblestone streets and beautiful ancient brickwork and blue painted shutters—closed. In fact, everything was closed up tight. And the streets were empty and silent. I was actually annoyed. Where was the action? The fun? The cafes, the French natives with all that *ooh la la!*? Where was the music? The wine? The chic shops?

I found the *boulangerie,* but just like everything else in this quiet village, it was closed. In fact, there was a little sign on the door saying they would not reopen until two in the afternoon. It was now noon. To me, this seemed insane and for a moment I considered going back down the hill and returning later, but then the prospect of climbing up the hill again made me decide against that. Instead, I went to the library. It was closed, *bien sûr.* I walked to the artisan soap shop. Closed. The pharmacy. Closed. The bank. Closed. In fact, the bank was permanently closed, shut down. There wasn't even an ATM machine.

This was indeed a small town. Nonetheless, I saw that there was a beauty salon! Ah, so perhaps their priorities were different. Money: not so important. Beauty: *very important*! I decided to visit the cathedral (which was open, cool and dark, and a nice relief after being out in the heat of the midday sun).

After a time, I continued to wander around the village. There was a ghostly silence over the place, but by walking slowly and listening more intently, I could hear the sounds of laughter and conversation. I peaked inside the lace curtains and I noticed the sound of clinking glasses and silverware and plates behind the almost completely closed shutters. And I realized—the good people of Auvillar were not out and about on the street, because they were inside enjoying their midday meal. For two hours. And later, I learned that sometimes after this meal and before going back to work, they took a little nap or at the very least, they lay down and relaxed.

And so, I relaxed. And then, it was two o'clock and I returned to the *boulangerie*, which was still not open yet, but a little line was beginning to form. No one seemed at all dismayed by this. In fact, we chatted and waited and after a while the proprietress opened the door and we all bought our bread or quiche or pastry.

Work to Live, Don't Live to Work

Later that evening, Cheryl Fortier, the director of Virginia Center for the Creative Arts at Auvillar (and a wonderful artist herself), invited everyone from the art colony to come to town to the local gallery to see a show of Christophe Gardner's beautiful photographs. There were many portraits of the local people, as well as the landscape—truly an homage to Auvillar. Everyone was there! The little gallery was filled with people laughing and drinking wine and enjoying the little appetizers. The crowd spilled out into the street and I couldn't help but think about what a difference this was from the quiet earlier in the day. There was such a sense of joyousness in the air, I imagined that their midday meal at home and their little naps certainly fortified the good people of Auvillar for a night on the town!

Now, I'm not suggesting that you walk into your supervisor's office and demand a two-hour lunch and a nap every day. I'm not even suggesting that you walk everywhere and find a particularly circuitous route. I'm not even suggesting you add colorful shutters to your windows and hang lace curtains. However, I am suggesting that you integrate this notion of the Secret Garden into your life. You'll see that by adding mystery and rest and privacy into your everyday world, you will feel better, stronger, and dare I say happier! And it's not so difficult to do.

Start by Dressing Up

Yes, I'm suggesting that you dress well—I don't mean you should wear an evening gown or a tuxedo, but something that makes you feel good about yourself. Something that is dignified and elegant, or something that is hip and sexy and edgy, and if that is who you are, you will begin your path toward happiness. *Joie de vivre.* When we walk out into the world wearing something that is just thrown on, something we feel slightly embarrassed about—say a pair of gray sweats, a faded T-shirt, and a pair of old sandals—we will not want to be seen. We will avoid running into people we know. We will avoid eye contact with the good-looking stranger at the wine store. In fact, suppose there really is a good-looking man in the wine store. He's hesitating over the bottles of Malbec. And there you are, about to grab the usual bottle. You actually happen to be a bit of an expert when it comes to Malbec and you could give him a few tips, begin a conversation, and who knows what else. But you look a mess! So when the gentleman in question asks about the Malbec, you might lower your head, point to your bottle, and quickly tell him this one is good, then scurry to the cash register before he can notice the tear in the inside seam of your sweatpants!

Okay, this is an extreme example, and I'm sure you never dress this way, but you get the idea. What you wear is part of your Secret Garden. It allows you to feel confident. If we were to play a rerun of this scenario, you, the heroine in this story, would now be wearing a pair of great-fitting jeans and a simple clean white T-shirt. And you've added a small bright blue scarf that you've tied around your neck like a choker with the knot jauntily placed to the side. You're carrying with you this really cute vintage straw bag that your grandmother gave you. Oh, and your sandals? They're very strappy. And they're red. Perhaps they match your red lipstick. Or maybe you're wearing no makeup at all, but your hair is shiny and clean.

Now, when the man who wants to buy a bottle of Malbec approaches you, there's no sudden panic, no need to run in the other direction. In fact, you may find yourself exchanging a delightful conversation on the intricacies of how the soil plays an important role in the flavor of the wine and you introduce this man to the idea of *terroir*—how each wine carries with it the DNA of its own origins, its homeland, so to speak—the rocks and minerals and rain water and winds of its region. And perhaps you exchange more talk of wine. Perhaps this encounter leads to a coffee or to meeting up with a group at a local restaurant/bar and, if you are a Frenchwoman, a dinner party.

Polly-Vous Français?

Polly Freeman Lyman is the author of the very popular blog Polly-Vous Français?—which gets 250,000 annual hits worldwide and was recently honored by *Budget Travel* as one of the top ten expat Paris blogs. Polly was a French literature major who first visited Paris in 1973. She was smitten and she spent the next thirty years failing at trying to masquerade as a Frenchwoman in the United States. This included stints of smoking Gauloises and even wearing espadrilles in the heart of the New England winter. She's now writing her memoir, *How to Not Become a Parisienne in 12 Easy Lessons.* Oh, and did I mention? She's a very funny gal. Here's what she has to say about *joie de vivre:*

> From my years of living in Paris, I learned that *joie de vivre* is a special way of delighting in the moment, of savoring the details of everyday existence. And, in return, creating them, as well: use the silver tableware every day, drink your morning coffee from that exquisite porcelain cup, acknowledge the handsome

> good looks of the gentleman walking past you on the sidewalk. Keep flowers on the table. Have something witty or interesting to add to a conversation. And never, ever wear sweatpants in public: Life is too short not to contribute to the *joie de vivre* of the admiring world around you!

When we protect and nourish our Secret Gardens, it becomes easier to draw a line and delineate our public persona from our private persona. In the comfort of our own home, we can retreat to our private chambers, spend the afternoon in bed with a good book, wearing just a robe or a nightgown or even sweats. Having indulged in this private time, we are rested and relaxed, so that when it's time to go out in the world, we're ready to dress for show.

What We Can Learn About *Joie de Vivre* from Paul Newman

I grew up not far from Westport, Connecticut, where the movie star Paul Newman and his wife, Joanne Woodward, lived. My mother was a bit of an outlaw in her own way and liked nothing better than to spend a Saturday afternoon driving down private roads and looking at mansions. Whenever she saw a sign that said NO TRESPASSING: PRIVATE ROAD, she couldn't resist breaking the law and driving down the road. As a child, I was completely mortified and screamed at her that we were going to get arrested, but my protests just seemed to encourage her.

We were always on the lookout for movie stars. There were quite a few of them living in Westport in those days (as well as today). But we specifically were trying to find Paul Newman's house. My mother was in love with Paul Newman. She saw herself as being the undiscovered Joanne Woodward and told me that they actually looked alike. Maybe they did, but was this any reason to track down Paul Newman? And what was her intention once we found him? Did she think she was going to seduce him and convince him to leave his beloved Joanne? I was only ten years old and all these questions left me feeling a little confused and worried for my mother, for Paul, and for Joanne.

Usually, our expeditions led to nothing more than a fun outing, but one day, thanks to some directions from a very friendly shopkeeper in Westport's pink-painted Incredible Bookstore, we actually found the Newman house. We were a bit surprised by the ordinariness of it. It was nice, but after all, it was just a house. There were no castle turrets, no moats. We sat in the car and stared at it and wondered where Paul was and whether he was inside or not and if Joanne was at home—perhaps in the backyard, doing some gardening, rehearsing lines for a new play? But no, the place was absolutely still. "Maybe they're in Hollywood," my mother said, starting up the engine to our Ford Pinto. And then it happened. A bright red Volkswagen Beetle sped by us, and my mother screamed, "That's him! That's him!" She let down the emergency hand brake, revved the engine, and we were on our way, chasing down Paul Newman. Oh, and she was sure it was Paul Newman because everyone in town knew he had taken an ordinary Volkswagen Beetle and put a very special, very fast Porsche engine in it for the express purpose of escaping nosy fans, specifically my mother and me. We tried to catch up with him. He turned a corner and the engine roared and we went in pursuit, down the private road with the speed bumps, the two of us practically propelled out of our seats in chase, and then finally we came to a little fork in the road. And he was gone. Nowhere to be seen. Paul Newman had escaped us!

I like to tell this story, which I admit I've hardly embellished at all, not so much because of our close encounter with Paul or because of our brush with greatness, but because we left the chase admiring Paul more than ever. Paul Newman could certainly afford the biggest, fanciest most expensive car that Hollywood money could buy (this was even before his salad dressing and popcorn success), but he didn't want to do anything obvious. Rather, he tucked a powerful, speed-racing engine inside a modest little VW bug. This is probably one of the best examples I can think of living happily and living hidden. There are no jealous stares and no envious backlash when one lives this way. It is about surviving by one's wits. It is about being clever and confident and perhaps thumbing one's nose at over-the-top consumerism and assumptions about wealth.

Paul Newman taught me that maintaining one's privacy—one's Secret Garden—doesn't mean you're rude or snobby. You can have fun and still be a very private person.

Private Road, No Trespassing

Your Secret Garden might even be something that simply lives and grows within your heart. It is true that the French do not reveal themselves as quickly or as easily as Americans. And while you may not want to stop being so friendly and open-hearted and accepting, you might rethink the occasional urge to give too much of yourself. There are times when you are drained, exhausted, and rather than taking care of yourself, lying down or going into a library, a church, a quiet cafe, you get on the phone with a girlfriend and talk. Perhaps you talk too much and out of your sense of fragility you reveal too much. And rather than finding this talking session a release, you hang up feeling as if some essential part of your being has been compromised. Your secrets are out there in the universe and you have not had the time or the space to come to your private resolution. What I am suggesting here is to find balance in your life. Take a cue from the French people in Auvillar who close the curtains, spend time with their family, enjoy a leisurely meal and rest, so that they are filled with energy and goodwill and confidence that they will then share with the world, without feeling they have overshared or given too much of themselves.

In the end, the Secret Garden is yours to create. It is your own special place in your life. If you tend it, care for it, protect it, and visit it often, your Secret Garden will give back to you all the fruits of your labor, and great joy.

French Lessons

CONSIDER WHETHER you are out of balance. Do you spend all your energies on your job and leave little time in your life for the ordinary little pleasures of life? Is there a way you can take a three-day weekend and truly get away from it all? It's important for your peace of mind to balance work with pleasure by resting and restoring your body, mind, and spirit on a regular basis. Perhaps you can't close the shutters and take an afternoon nap every day, but you can certainly turn down a few requests for your time and indulge in something you find peaceful and replenishing.

Ask yourself whether you are saving your life for a rainy day. And look at the ordinary things that you might enjoy right now, such as the good china, fresh flowers on your table, that delicious bit of chocolate. Wear your grandmother's pearls. Take the diamonds out of the safe deposit box. This is all about living for today and being present to the beauty each ordinary moment has to offer you.

Create a Secret Garden that is yours and yours alone. Once you decide what, where, when, and how you take refuge in this secret garden, protect it from intruders (turn off the phone and be sure to keep the computer out of your sacred space).

Take the stairs whenever possible and try to walk everywhere—or at least as much as you can. Try parking your car in the center of town; you'll enjoy accomplishing your errands more if you walk from shop to shop. Be sure to bring a light canvas bag in your purse. This idea of walking is no small thing, because it will help you find your sense of being grounded. It will add to your confidence, especially if you dress for presentation. You know you look lovely and you will welcome unexpected encounters. By dressing well when you go out, you also create a clear delineation between your exterior world and your interior world. Your Secret Garden is the place where you can wear anything—or nothing at all!

Resist the urge to dish too much or talk about all your private business. While we might feel good when we get to share our worries and insecurities, we might later feel a bit undressed and even more insecure! So, it's important to switch the conversation and ask your companion about their life.

Protect your privacy—in your home as well as in your heart. Sometimes you need to hide away your heart as well as hiding away your Porsche engine inside an unassuming VW Bug.

Take a tip from Frenchwomen. They seldom give "tours" of their house and they often keep much hidden. When you have a party, it's okay to only use the main room, then you're not worried people are looking through your things. And you won't find a couple making out on top of the coats in your bedroom—not that something like that has ever happened in your house!

CHAPTER FOUR

Recipes for Joie de Vivre

À vos amours.
(To your loves.)
—A FRENCH TOAST

IF HAPPINESS COMES from an experience that we share with others, then certainly the dinner table is a place where we can find a whole lot of *joie de vivre*. This is especially true if we enjoy our meals like the French, *en famille*. When you eat with your family and friends, the dinner table is not simply a place where you eat food. No, it's the place where generations have shared the stories of their daily lives, where we've hashed out schedules and laughed at a child's joke. It's the place where a teenage girl announced that she was against the Iraq War and that she wanted to spend the summer in Europe. It's the place where arguments erupt and words fly. It's the place where someone throws down a napkin in a huff, stands, and leaves the room—only to return later, feeling a little shy, in need of something sweet, ready for that dessert, perhaps an apple tart and a piece of chocolate, if you please.

It's the place where romances are formed, and kisses are stolen. It's the place where someone's knee presses up against someone else's knee. It's the place where your old boyfriend from years past gets a little tipsy one night and kisses you right on the mouth. It's the place where you tell your husband you are pregnant. And yes, it's the place where you drink and eat and cry and talk and laugh and eat some more.

Oh, and speaking of "eating," the French actually never use the word "eating" or *manger* for people, but only animals. When the French want to talk about people eating, they will use the verb *diner,* to dine. How civilized!

But, as Americans, many of us have lost this sacred ritual. In fact, a recent study shows that only 28 percent of Americans sit down to eat together for the evening meal compared to 92 percent of French families who dine together each night. When you realize that the evening meal is about so much more than just eating—excuse me, dining—you can really begin to understand what we are at risk of losing.

Romance Starts Here

Chris Rock is a funny man, but the other day he said something so moving and so revealing. He was a guest on *The Rachael Ray Show.* She asked him whether he remembered every woman he ever dated before he married (apparently there were quite a few), and he answered no, that he didn't remember every woman he ever dated. But he said he did remember every woman who ever cooked for him. How romantic—and how revealing.

And why is the sit-down dinner so important for the French? The entire culture depends on it. Yes, this is where romance begins. In fact, children often meet each other for the first time at their families' dinner parties. The neighbors' children come along and a lifelong romance takes root that night, as the children simply play together. Then years pass and they grow up to be teenagers and gradually that friendship deepens and blossoms into something more mature.

The Secret to Love: Roquefort Soufflé

Sometimes the road from friendship to romance can be a little confusing.

How do we let someone know that we're attracted to him or her and want to get to know him or her better? And is it really true that making a delicious meal for someone can lead to love? Well, yes. *Absolument!*

My friend and editor, Audrey, is a total Francophile. She recently married a wonderful gentleman named Stephen, who shares with her a love of good food and good wine. In fact, their romance began over Roquefort soufflé.

She met Stephen at her home during a Sunday afternoon "apartment sale" where she had invited everyone in her building—that's about five hundred apartments—to come and see everything she wanted to sell in order to get ready for a major renovation. She had already done the kitchen, so as a lure she told everyone to "come see a fully renovated kitchen," but she also added—and this is very French—"refreshments will be served." Certainly, Stephen came to see her kitchen, but the refreshments made him linger a while—along with the fact, I'm sure, that Audrey is a beautiful woman. And she has the lithe and graceful figure of a ballerina. That's no surprise since she actually was a ballerina for many years in New York City, dancing for the Mercury Ballet Company.

It was a warm spring day and so Audrey served a Casa Julia and a Casa Lapostolle white wine from Chile. She tells me it's surprisingly good and only costs about seven dollars a bottle. She set up a nice table in her main room with the chilled wine, real glassware (something Frenchwomen always do!), grapes, and an assortment of good cheeses. To this she added a vase of fresh flowers and some pretty napkins. It's these small but very simple gestures that can truly bring a sense of elegance to your table.

Audrey sold a lot of furniture that day, as well as rugs and other things, but she was a little surprised by how few people partook of her lovely refreshments! She was definitely disappointed by this; however, Stephen was the exception and this is why she immediately took a liking to him! Her apartment was full of people and she was negotiating, selling, and handling various transactions. While all this was going on, Stephen poured himself a glass of wine and patiently waited for the perfect opportunity to engage Audrey in a conversation. He was very attracted to her, and a discussion about the renovation process gave him a chance to spend some time with her. Audrey just imagined that he was simply interested in all the details. He wanted to know what designer she had chosen, why she had decided on all the specifics. Finally, he told her that he wanted to know all this because he, too, had renovated his apartment. "Would she like to see?" he asked.

Bien sûr! And then he invited her over for a tour. Little

did she know that this "tour" would include dinner, let alone a beautiful homemade Roquefort soufflé!

I love this story and knew right away that I had to track down the recipe for Roquefort soufflé. And so, I met with Audrey and Stephen's friend Susan in Paris. Susan has lived in Paris since 2003 when she left the world of advertising in Southern California to move to France. Susan and her late husband were good friends with Stephen. And even though years have passed and Susan now lives in Paris and Stephen in New York, they have continued their friendship.

Today, Susan lives in the apartment of her dreams in Saint-Germain-des-Prés with her life companion, Wolfgang. The couple was featured in *House Hunters International* and they're often recognized as they travel throughout the world. Still, even though she is far away from her old friend, they talk on the phone and e-mail and she's always ready to lend a helping hand. And that help includes recipes for *joie de vivre.* When she heard that Stephen had become smitten with a beautiful neighbor in his building, and that he had invited her to see his apartment, Susan immediately sent off her "guaranteed-to-make-an-impression soufflé recipe." And you know, it worked!

Stephen prepared as much as possible ahead of time, but to his surprise and delight, Audrey loves being in the kitchen and so making the dish became a joint effort and the beginnings of real true love bloomed from there. In 2005, the two couples—Audrey and Stephen and Susan and Wolfgang—celebrated New Year's Eve in Paris and then in July 2008 they met again to celebrate Audrey and Stephen's very elegant wedding in Italy.

And now for the recipe . . . but, handle with care, because this dish could lead to a whole lot of *joie de vivre*, and even wedding bells!

✦ ✦ ✦

Susan's Roquefort Soufflé

Makes 4 servings.

Preparation time: 1½ hours

Baking time: 45 minutes–1 hour

6 tablespoons butter
2 tablespoons fine breadcrumbs
6 tablespoons flour
1½ cups milk
6 egg yolks
¾ cup Roquefort or bleu cheese, crumbled
⅓ cup cream cheese
7 egg whites
1½ tablespoons cornstarch

1. Preheat oven to 375°F.
2. Coat a large soufflé dish with butter. Sprinkle breadcrumbs to cover.
3. Melt the butter in saucepan over low heat. Add the flour and stir frequently over low heat for about 5 minutes. Do not let brown.
4. Bring milk with added pinch of salt to boil.
5. Add to flour-butter mixture.
6. When fully incorporated and very thick, beat in egg yolks, one at a time.

7. Add Roquefort (or bleu cheese) and cream cheese, stirring over low heat to incorporate well and then set aside.
8. Whip egg whites with cornstarch until stiff peaks form.
9. Fold ¼ of whites into cheese mixture.
10. Fold in remaining whites.
11. Spoon into soufflé dish.
12. Bake for 45 minutes to one hour or until tester comes out clean.

Lunchtime in the South of France

My French friend Béatrice is a high-powered executive in the medical field. She graduated from Yale University and speaks fluent English. Today, she lives and works in Southwest France in the beautiful city of Toulouse. I stayed with her last fall at her lovely home not far from the center of the city and was so lucky to experience authentic French hospitality.

Béatrice works from home and she's very successful, but also very busy! Still, I was amazed and impressed at how she asked me to return home from my day of touring Toulouse to have lunch with her. In the middle of her working day, she stopped and made a homemade quiche with a deliciously fresh salad for me. The quiche was so creamy—just taken out of the oven as I was arriving home, piping hot and so delicious! Honestly, I've eaten many a quiche in my time and I occasionally make my own quiche, but this quiche that Béatrice made will hold a place in my memory as the best quiche I've ever eaten. This is not because the quiche was so delicious (and it was truly very, very delicious), but because of the generosity of this meal. And even more than this, it was the sense of improvised elegance. There was nothing fussy or overly orchestrated about my little luncheon with Béatrice, but the simplicity and beauty of this meal felt like a true luxury to me. And this was certainly an example of *joie de vivre.* It was a shared experience full of laughter and love.

And here, Béatrice has given me the recipe:

✦ ✦ ✦

My Family Quiche from Béatrice

Makes 4 to 6 servings.

Size of the pie pan: 10 inches

Preparation time: 10–15 minutes (without the pastry crust; for the dough, add another 15 minutes and 20 minutes to rest in the fridge)

Cooking time: 30 minutes

1 already-made pastry crust—or follow this recipe:

For the pastry crust:
3½ ounces softened butter cut in small pieces
7 ounces flour
1 egg
3 teaspoons milk
salt

1. In a bowl, put flour and salt, then add the butter and mix with fingers.
2. Add the egg and keep on mixing with fingers. Add a drop of milk so the mix forms a ball.

3. Let rest in the fridge for minimum half an hour. (It can be prepared earlier in the day. In that case let it stand about 20 minutes out of the fridge before rolling it.)
4. When ready to use, take the dough out and using a rolling pin, roll it on a piece of cooking paper. Place it in the pan with the paper.
5. Preheat the oven to 460°F.

For the filling of the quiche:

4 egg yolks
4 egg whites
1 cup cream
3½ ounces shredded Swiss cheese
7 ounces bacon cut in small bits
7 ounces cooked ham sliced, and cut in small squares
Pepper (1 pinch)
Nutmeg (1 pinch)

1. In a bowl, mix the egg yolks and the cream. Add the shredded cheese, pepper, and nutmeg. (Usually you don't need to add salt, as the bacon, ham, and cheese are already salted.)
2. Beat the whites until hard.
3. Carefully incorporate the whites (without breaking) in the bowl containing yolks, cream, and cheese.
4. In the pan, on the unbaked crust, place bacon and ham.
5. Pour the filling in the crust.
6. Place low in the oven for 30 minutes.

Serve with a green salad.

The wonderful thing about making quiche is that you can also prepare it ahead of time and serve it later. We often think of dinner parties as being a little daunting, but the French don't believe in that either/or mentality—either microwaving a frozen dinner or going all out and creating an elaborate eight-course meal. Rather, they will prepare one lovely "centerpiece" dish a day in advance. (A quiche can work well as a main dish.) And then they will add to this a few simple things such as a lovely salad, a soup that compliments the main dish, a fresh baguette and a cheese course, followed by dessert, coffee, and finally a digestif such as Armagnac or perhaps a nice cognac.

"Cake" for Dinner

I met up with Isabelle, who we met in chapter 1, in Paris recently. You may remember that she's a friend of my friend Tania. The three of us went out to dinner and got to talking about love and life and, of course, food. Isabelle comes from the countryside near St. Etienne. She did her studies in Lyon and has traveled quite a bit, and like most of the French people I've met, she loves to cook when she has the time (she's very busy with her career in personal development, often traveling for work and visiting various companies). She did tell me that she comes from a family of cooks and so she offered me this wonderful family recipe for salted cake.

Now, you might not think of cake as something you'd have with dinner, but in this case it is! And what's really great about this is if you're planning a get-together, it's easy to prepare in advance, leaving you more time to spend with your guests. I found that you could keep Isabelle's salted cake in the fridge for a couple of days and the taste was even more fantastic! It can be served hot or at room temperature, although never cold. It's perfect to serve at a sit-down dinner party, as well as at a buffet because you can preslice the cake and it's very easy to handle. It's very delicious and very healthy. I love this recipe!

✦ ✦ ✦

Isabelle's Salted Cake with Bleu Cheese and Prunes

Makes 4 to 6 servings.

Preparation time: 15 minutes

Baking time: 45 minutes

7 ounces flour
3 eggs
⅓ cup whole milk
⅓ cup olive oil
1 package baking yeast
5 ounces bleu cheese, if possible bleu de Bresse
10 prunes (dried fruits, not fresh plums)
3½ ounces grated gruyere cheese
¾ ounce butter
Salt and pepper

1. Cut the bleu cheese in small diced pieces. Take the stones out of the prunes, cut the prunes in small pieces, as well. Roll all these pieces in flour.
2. Preheat the oven to 350°F.
3. Mix in a bowl flour and yeast and beaten eggs with

salt and pepper. Add oil and milk, and mix well. Then incorporate the diced cheese and prunes.

4. Pour this pastry dough into the mold and bake for around 45 minutes in the oven. Check the baking by sticking the cake with the blade of a knife. It has to come out dry. If not, cook a little longer.
5. Let it cool down for 5 minutes before unmolding. Serve at ambient temperature.

It's really lovely to serve with a crunchy green salad.

Teasing the Palate

And what can you serve to your guests while you're arranging the last-minute preparations for your dinner party? The French believe in not filling up before a meal, but rather saving the appetite for the dinner. And yet, it's important to waken up the senses in preparation for the meal. The French expression for this is *amuse-gueule.* I love the sound of this because it's about amusing the mouth or the gullet. It's really just an expression for what we would call a cocktail snack. I often hear the French call it *grignottes* or "nibblies," which is English, but then I never hear English speakers use this expression, so it's a little confusing. All this is to say, the French do like to tease the palate before a fine meal. In Paris, they will often start with champagne, but in Auvillar, during the summer we would begin with a kir aperitif (crème de cassis and a dry white wine). To make a kir royale, you just use champagne instead of white wine. For our *amuse-gueule,* we generally served olives or salted nuts. But one night, Cheryl prepared a plate of cherry tomatoes that had been coated in carmelized sugar and then, using a toothpick, dipped in toasted sesame seeds. It was just a small plate, and easy to make, but very delicious.

You see, the idea here is to tease the palate and coax the hunger. The actual first course of a meal might be a bit of soup. On our first night in Auvillar, Cheryl gave us each a plate with a fig (from our very own tree) split open and sprinkled with crumbled chèvre and decorated with mint leaves. Another night, we had a little slice of foie gras on some greens. Then there's more wine and then the main course, which might be a small portion of fresh fish and some vegetables. More wine. Oh, and water from the clear water bottle that always sits at the table. Then comes the cheese course (with a lovely baguette and a selection of different cheeses—France has over five hundred), and finally the dessert and when that's done, espresso. Everything is served on small plates, one at a time. You can see why the typical dinner party takes hours and hours!

Cheryl Fortier is a wonderful cook, a very fine artist, and a woman who certainly knows how to create a festive dinner party. She grew up in French-speaking Canada and now lives in Vancouver with her husband, John, a writer and a photographer. She hosted many a memorable fête at Auvillar—some quite casual and some more formal.

✦ ✦ ✦

Foie Gras on Toasts with Onion Confit from Cheryl Fortier

Makes 6 servings.

Preparation time: 10 minutes

Cooking time: 30 minutes

1 can foie gras, refrigerated
1 fresh artisan baguette, cut into ¼-inch slices
Olive oil

For the confit:

1½ pounds yellow onions
1 tablespoon olive oil
1 tablespoon butter, unsalted
2 tablespoons sugar
¼ cup red wine
2 teaspoons fresh thyme, chopped
A small pinch nutmeg
Salt and pepper to taste

1. Preheat oven to 325°F. Brush each side of baguette slices with a little olive oil. Toast until golden, about 10 minutes per side. Cool completely and store in an airtight container if not using immediately.
2. Heat butter and olive oil in a heavy skillet on medium heat. Add onions, reduce heat slightly, add sugar, and cook slowly until soft but not browned, approximately 15 minutes. Stir occasionally.

3. Increase heat to medium-high and add wine. Cook, stirring occasionally until wine is absorbed and the onions are golden, approximately 15 minutes. Add thyme, nutmeg, salt, and pepper.

When ready to serve:

Arrange toasts on a platter. Remove foie gras from jar or tin. Tip: If it's in a tin, open both ends and gently push foie gras through. Remove excess fat and slice foie gras with a warm, sharp knife or unflavored dental floss. It is best to work quickly as the foie gras becomes soft as it warms.

Place slices of foie gras on toasts and serve with a bowl of onion confit. Garnish with small sprigs of fresh thyme.

What I love about this recipe is that it's very tasty and impressive, but actually easy to prepare and not labor intensive. If you take a look at your local gourmet food shop, you'll find that there's a selection of wonderful prepared foods that you can mix and match with homemade items. Trader Joe's, Whole Foods, Dean & Deluca, and the gourmet section of almost any supermarket are all great places to find an unusual or exotic prepared item that adds panache to any dinner.

Eau-de-Vie (Water of Life)

For a Frenchwoman or man, wine is not simply this drink that tastes delicious and makes you feel good. The French know that the wine grown from grapes in a particular region will carry inside its taste a whole history of that region—

from rainstorms to droughts, from long hot summers to early frosty autumn mornings. All these changes will go into the soil and the soul of the grape. And when a wine is produced from a family's own fruit tree, surely it carries with it a sense of that family's history, their connection to the land and an undeniable connection between the past, the present, and the future.

Recently, Tania told me about this special drink called eau-de-vie. This wine is a digestif made in Normandy from apples. Her grandparents had an apple field and they used to make cider from these apples and then distill them to make the eau-de-vie. When Tania was born, her father reserved some of the bottles to be enjoyed at a special occasion such as her first Communion or wedding. The older the drink, the better it is. And so her father saved bottles for her, her sister, and her brother, each on the day they were born. When Tania marries, you can imagine how much *joie de vivre* a sip of this apple cider will bring to her and of course to her entire family!

The Perfect Palate Cleanser

Melanie Griot had a grandmother who was a Julia Child kind of woman in Provence. This is where Melanie grew up. She now lives in New York City. She's a writer and presently she works as a waitress—and has written some very funny essays about her adventures in the restaurant world. She's around food a lot and she loves to eat! Here's what she told me in a recent e-mail:

> I never got that business of skipping breakfast. Eating is the reason I wake up. In northwestern

> France, where I come from, there is a trick to six-course dinners. First, they last for a while, at least three hours. And it's not so bad with wine to mellow out the recalcitrant mother-in-law or the teenage boy sitting next to you. Not that you'd get wasted . . . with all that food, it's hardly possible. You see, the French drink to eat and vice versa. Muscadet accompanies oysters, sauternes (a sweet white wine) goes with foie gras, and a pinot noir from Burgundy is a natural when it comes to pork. Still, it's a lot of food . . . so about halfway through the dinner, we take a break. *Trou normand*, as it's called, involves a scoop of apple sorbet with a shot of Calvados (apple brandy). It helps with digestion and cleanses your palate (sixty proof) for the remaining courses. We wouldn't want to miss out on a stinky cheese.

Le trou normand can be translated as a "the hole from Normandy" and the expression *faire un trou* simply means to take a break in between courses.

While it's easy to find apple sorbet in stores in France, you might have some difficulty finding it here in the States. Still, a lemon sorbet will work just as well with the Calvados. And actually you can serve an impressive palate cleanser by just serving a bit of homemade or storebought sorbet in not-too-sweet flavors such as lime, lemon, or mint.

So you see, serving a palate cleanser really involves very little effort and provides great pleasure. If you're serving a meal that has many courses, why not surprise your guests with a course in the middle of a little scoop of lemon sorbet and a little bit of brandy poured into the dish? It's sure to delight and enliven the meal. And it prepares your guests for the next course and definitely adds a lot of *joie de vivre* to the dinner table.

I just have to add a little side note here. Melanie is slender. Yes, she enjoys all this delicious French food and she will take part in the five-hour dinner party when she visits her family back home, but somehow she stays slim. I can only imagine that it's the fresh food, the small but delicious portions, taking lots of time, never skipping breakfast, and perhaps even that *trou normand* that helps her keep her girlish figure!

✦ ✦ ✦

Le Trou Normand with Melon from Melanie Griot

1. Take a small melon, slice it in the middle, and take out the seeds.
2. Pour a shot of Calvados in the hole or the middle of the melon.

The melon *trou* can also be served as an appetizer. And Melanie tells me there are lots of regional *trou.* For example, there's *trou gascon,* which is simply melon with berries (strawberries or raspberries work well) served with cognac or Armagnac. You might also like to try *trou champenois.* Simply add some *marc de champagne,* a brandy made from grapes, to a dish of champagne sorbet. I found several excellent recipes on the Internet for champagne sorbet, along with rhubarb, cranberry, tangerine, and plum sorbet. So use your imagination and have fun.

In fact, the *melon trou* can also be served as an appetizer.

A Family Recipe from Ile de Ré

Not too long ago, I was sitting at my Weight Watchers meeting on Cape Cod, listening to the ladies talk, when suddenly I heard the unmistakable lilt of a French accent. I quickly turned my head and blurted out, "Are you French!?" Magali, a beautiful, smart, and funny French lady, looked at me, smiling slightly with a little twinkle in her eyes as if she found my unbridled enthusiasm very amusing, and then she calmly replied, "Why, yes. Of course I'm French."

As it turns out, Magali was born on the island Ile de Ré, which is in the *département* Charente-Maritime in the southwest of France, between Bordeaux and Brittany. Magali comes from a restaurant family and, in fact, her uncle is Chef Daniel Masse, the owner of the restaurant Le Chat Botté.

She has offered her family recipe for the traditional French crepe.

✦ ✦ ✦

Les Crepes from Magali

Makes 20–25 crepes.

Preparation time: 10 minutes

Cooking time: 5 minutes

4 cups milk
7 eggs
12 ounces flour
1 tablespoon orange zest

½ teaspoon orange blossom (if available) or ½ teaspoon rum or almond extract, according to taste.

1 ounce melted butter

1. Mix flour and milk.
2. Add eggs and zest. (The batter has to be very smooth and silky, but not too thick, and not too liquidy.)
3. Use a medium pan, a pancake pan, or a crepe pan.
4. Dip a piece of paper towel in the melted butter, and spread the butter all over the pan each time you make a new crepe.
5. Use a medium-size dipper for the batter, and spread the mix all over the pan.
6. Wait until it gets bubbly and flip the crepe over for one more minute on the other side.
7. When the crepe has a nice golden color, remove it from the pan, put it on a plate or flat dish, and sprinkle the crepe with sugar.
8. Start over, until there's no more batter left.

The best way to eat crepes is with sugar, jam, preserves, Nutella, or honey. It's also fine to eat the crepes with your fingers. Fold the crepe in two, then in two again, and you have a triangle.

Yes, crepes are a fun finger food. That's why children love crepes!

Sunshine on a Rainy Day

My friend Mary Kelly always wears a beret. She's an American, with—as she says—a *soupçon* of French in her DNA. She's also a fantastic cook and baker. I'll never forget how she once brought a lemon cake she had baked to my creative writing workshop at New York University. This was my "Proust class," in which I asked my students to bring their favorite dish to share and then write a story inspired by the sensory pleasure and childhood memories that the dish evoked for them.

She told me that while there are many wonderful recipes for lemon cake and you can find your own on the Internet or in many cookbooks, she herself makes this cake so often, her friends have begun to call it the Mary Kelly Lemon Cake.

I can understand why. Picture, if you will, the slightly drab little classroom in lower Manhattan on that cold and gray rainy winter's night. There we are, presented with this little yellow cake, very plain-looking except for the glistening, crunchy-looking topping made from granulated sugar and lemon juice. Well, the students and I had one little bite of that seemingly plain cake and suddenly the overwhelming sensation of pure sunshine and lemony goodness burst forth into the room. There were so many smiles. And then, laughter. So much *joie de vivre*! Yes, Mary's lemon cake brought a warm summer's day right to our door, and in that moment, all the winter gloom seemed to disappear.

I love teaching my "Proust class" because yes, it's fun and a bit of a party, but also because I find it revives and awakens all the senses and the most inspired stories emerge from the experience. Certainly, Mary's lemon cake ignited several stories that night and I suspect if you make it and then sit down to write or draw or paint or dance or play music, you too will find yourself feeling very creative! That's the power of a little cake you make from scratch.

✦ ✦ ✦

The Mary Kelly Lemon Cake

Makes 12 servings.

Preparation time: 15 minutes

Baking time: 30–35 minutes

Serve this cake while it's still slightly warm, topped with unsweetened whipped cream. This cake is best enjoyed the same day, so do not save any for the next day.

1 cup all-purpose flour
¾ teaspoon baking powder
¼ teaspoon baking soda
Pinch of salt
4 tablespoons unsalted butter, softened
¾ cup sugar
1 large egg (or 2 small eggs)
⅓ cup plain Greek yogurt, thinned with a little milk (any plain yogurt or a mild lemon-flavored yogurt will work)
Freshly grated lemon zest from one whole lemon

For the crunchy topping:

½ cup sugar (or enough to create a syrupy consistency)
Lemon juice of one whole lemon

1. Preheat oven to 350°F.
2. Sift together flour, baking powder, baking soda, and salt, and set aside.
3. In a large bowl, cream together butter and sugar with an electric mixer or by hand until light and fluffy. Add egg and beat at high speed for 1 minute or vigorously by hand. Alternately add yogurt and flour mixture in three additions, with mixer at low speed or stirring by hand. Stir in lemon zest.
4. Turn batter into a buttered and floured 8 inch springform pan, smoothing the top of batter with a spatula. Bake in the center of the oven for 30 to 35 minutes, or until a skewer inserted into the center of cake comes out clean.
5. Before cake is finished baking, in a small bowl combine sugar and lemon juice until it forms a syrupy consistency. Spread the syrupy topping evenly over cake as it comes from the oven. Set cake, in its pan, on a wire rack to cool. As the cake cools, the topping will harden and form a crust over the cake.

Merci for the Memories

When you think about it, some of the happiest moments in our lives are associated with the preparation, the serving, and the enjoyment of food. And this is because food engages all our senses—taste, touch, smell, sight, and *even sound.* (Consider the porterhouse steak as it sizzles on the patio barbeque or the almost imperceptible sound of bubbles rising and crashing before they explode at the lip of a champagne flute.) This place of intense awareness is where happiness begins—the moments in your life where you are fully engaged and your senses are completely awakened. And this is why cooking and food is a simple way to open the doors to joy.

When you bake a birthday cake for your husband—the one with his favorite chocolate frosting—you are creating an experience. If you make this cake every year, you are creating a tradition, and along with this comes memory and after a while, the emotional connection between this birthday cake and your love for him. Yes, eating the cake is an experience, but when you've sifted the flour and beat the eggs, when you've added the milk and vanilla extract, you become more connected to that cake, both physically and emotionally. On that frigid day in late January, on his thirty-seventh birthday, your husband walks in the door of the heated kitchen and he smiles at the sight of you, poised before the oven, gently testing the middle of the cake. He notices a powdery smudge of flour on your right cheek and the tiny bead of glistening sweat that lingers on your brow. All this effort for him, he muses, and in that moment a lifelong memory is formed in his mind. And the taste of that cake—after singing "Happy Birthday" and blowing out the thirty-eight candles (one for good luck)—well, it is all the more delicious because of the preparations leading up to this moment.

This is the true meaning of *joie de vivre.* It is all about this experience that connects you to your loved ones, your family and friends, and the world around you.

How sweet it is to receive the gift of homemade jam, especially if it comes from the raspberries grown in your friend's garden. Thelma, my friend and next door neighbor, gives me a jar of her homemade jam every summer. I love how she puts a little label on the glass jar with the family name and date. I love spreading the jam on toast on a cold winter's morning. The fragrance and taste immediately brings back the warmth of summer to me.

Most recently, my French tutor, Marceline, gave me and my husband a box of *tuiles* (little cookie crisps) that she had baked for us as a way of thanking us for inviting her to a dinner party. The *tuiles* were so crispy, light, and delicious, but I especially enjoyed them because we had talked about the cookies during the night of the party. My husband had never had them before and so her thoughtful gift also brought back fond memories of that evening.

When I was eight years old, my mother returned from a rather long stay in the hospital and our neighbor came over with a big covered dish of lasagna. She knew my mother wouldn't be up for cooking and so this dish was not only a get-well gift, but also a very thoughtful way of helping out during a troubled time. Here it is, almost fifty years later, and I can still conjure up the tangy taste of that tomato sauce and with it comes the memory of being part of a neighborhood and a world bigger than just my little family—filled with kindness and generosity, trust and grace.

Isabelle's *Grandmère*

You remember Isabelle—she's my Paris friend who gave me the salted cake recipe. We got to talking not too long ago and she told me how she comes from the countryside near St. Etienne. She did her studies in Lyon and has traveled quite a bit. She also loves to cook when she has time and comes from a family of wonderful cooks! Her grandma, Marie, who lives in the little village of Valprivas, has been baking goodies for Isabelle since she was a little girl. As a child, Isabelle declared that her favorite treat was her grandmother's croissants with nuts. Isabelle lives on her own in Paris, but for many, many years, whenever she visited Valprivas, she would ask her grandma to please make the croissants for her. And Grandma Marie was always delighted to oblige. The croissants always magically brought back so many wonderful childhood memories.

Isabelle's Grandma Marie is now eighty-nine and her eyesight is failing, and so she can't make croissants anymore. Still, Isabelle wanted to include her recipe in this book and so I am very honored to know that Isabelle's mother recently went to visit Grandma Marie in Valprivas and as she recited the recipe, Isabelle's mother wrote it all down—just for our American readers.

✦ ✦ ✦

Grandmère Marie's Croissants aux Noix

Makes 4 or 5 croissants.

10 to 12 walnuts
1½ slices of fresh ham, or about 3 ounces (not bacon, not dry ham)
Approximately 4 ounces grated Swiss cheese
2 cups clotted cream (One can replace the cream with milk, but it is not as nice!)

Basically, you have to make a filling (*farce* in French) for each croissant, and then bake them for 20 minutes. Very easy and so delicious.

1. Mix the walnuts and ham in an electric blender. Add the grated cheese and mix. Add the cream and blend it all together.
2. Let it rest for 2 hours (in the fridge or in a cool place, because of the cream).
3. Preheat the oven to 325°F.
4. Cut the croissants in half (lengthwise).
5. Put a large spoon (about 3 teaspoons) of filling on the lower part of each croissant and spread it. Then cover with the other upper half.
6. Bake for 20 minutes.

The croissants should not be too dry and the filling should remain soft.

Merci beaucoup, Grandmère Marie!

The Progressive Dinner Party

Now, after hearing from all these fabulous French cooks and learning about the French dinner party, you might think this is impossible to emulate in your own home, but actually American women are hosting successful parties all the time. I heard of a progressive dinner party in Plymouth, Massachusetts, where the families from within a particular neighborhood planned a dinner. Each couple chose what course they would prepare and the couples walked from house to house, progressively enjoying a ten-course meal. One couple was in charge of the *amuse-gueule* (small, but very tasty appetizer), another made a soup, another served wine, and so on. This is a fun and easy alternative to the sit-down dinner party. This actually reminded me a little bit of the Christmas Eve parties we had when I was growing up in Stamford. We would walk from house to house and then stand outside and sing Christmas carols. I remember that one father could play a mean harmonica and another played a little banjo. Afterwards, we were invited in for hot chocolate and other goodies. It was a great way to get to know our neighbors.

Cheryl Fortier told me about the Valentine's Day couples party that she planned. It's really a wonderful idea. Here's how it works: Each couple decides on what they will serve as their small-plate course and pairs it with a beverage and music. Cheryl explains:

> A few of us usually bring a small-plate dessert course, also. We let the hostess and host know our selections ahead of time so they can organize the courses in appropriate order and make the menu. We start early so that each couple has time to prep and serve their course and we have lots of time to enjoy it. Sometimes we dance between some of the courses. These dinners offer a license to be creative; in presentation of the small plates, table decor, choice of music, you could even dress in theme with your course!

And here's the program that was printed up for this festive occasion:

A Celebration of Food, Wine & Valentine

FEBRUARY 14

Miso Scallops on Pea Shoots
with Wasabi Aioli and Pickled Ginger
Prosecco di Valdobbiadene
MUSIC: Chet Baker's *Songs for Lovers*

Crab Ravioli with Truffled Beurre Blanc
Alsatian Pinot Gris
Alsatian Riesling

Chinese Snow Cones
(served on a lovely handmade wooden snow cone holder)
See Ya Later Ranch Riesling
MUSIC: Yo-Yo Ma's *Silk Road Journeys: When Strangers Meet*

Grilled Lamb Chops with Mint Sauce
Roasted Asparagus Spears
Syrah

The Grand Dessert Course:
Chocolat Pots de Crème
Crème Brûlée
Chocolate Gâteau with Fresh Strawberries
Opimian Ten-Year-Old Tawny Port
Van Gogh Espresso Vodka
Cabernet Franc
MUSIC: Carla Bruni's "Quelqu'un M'adit"

French Lessons

TAKE THE PRESSURE out of planning a dinner party by adding to your repertoire a few dishes that are tried and true and easy to prepare a day or two in advance, so you'll never feel overwhelmed the day of the party. Find out what sort of prepared foods you can purchase from your local gourmet food shops that will impress guests and make dinner party preparations easier.

Create new memories among your family and friends by preparing their favorite foods or dishes that they have come to associate with a visit to your home. Honor birthdays and other celebrations—not by buying some expensive gift, but by giving the gift of your time and effort and the thoughtfulness of a delicious dish.

Take care of your neighbors who are ill or in need of a little help by bringing them a covered dish. This is how a true sense of community is formed.

Enlist the help of your friends and start with small potluck-style parties that will build your confidence so you can tackle bigger, more elaborate dinner parties. Perhaps join or start a dinner party club with couples and singles you know and like and want to get to know better.

And sit down with your family at least once a week to a real meal. Light some candles. Play some soft music. This will signify that you are sharing an age-old ritual.

Oh, and even when you're not using it, keep the dining room table free of clutter. After all, it is a sacred space.

CHAPTER FIVE

Zen à la Française

From a recent e-mail:

Bonjour, Je suis en vacances du 26/7 au 24/8/2010.
(Hello, I will be on vacation from July 26 to August 24, 2010.)

BACK IN THE DAY—1974, to be exact—someone gave me a copy of Ram Dass's book *Be Here Now.* I was a senior at Bard College. I sat in my little dorm room on Annandale Road, surrounded by the purple, pink, and orange Indian print bedspreads lining my walls and as I listened to Joni Mitchell's *Blue* album on the stereo. I read all about Zen and the concept of being present in any given moment. Zen meditation. This may sound like something that's not so hard to do—to be present. But, as I was reading about being present and trying to be present, my mind slipped off into other worrisome places involving reading two hundred pages of Chaucer's *Canterbury Tales* before Friday and writing that paper on the Lost Generation that was already overdue, and then there was the fact that I still hadn't found a boyfriend and was way behind on the quest to lose my virginity before graduation!

Still, I must say the notion of being mindful and present, without being grasping or in a state of constant dissatisfaction, sounded very good indeed. I liked the idea of sitting and doing nothing and the dichotomy of finding discipline, while remaining free of mind-numbing habits. I decided right then and there that this thing called Zen was just what I needed. And I must say that *Be Here Now*—this crazy quilt of a book with lots of CAPITAL LETTERS and swirling patterns and trippy drawings—made swallowing the idea of serious daily meditation and developing a "practice" by detaching from the material world actually seem kind of fun and wild. Maybe even *wacky*!

Clouds in My Coffee

Still, it wasn't until I got to Paris the following year that I truly began to come close to an understanding of Zen. I believe I discovered Zen in a Paris cafe. I had very little money, and couldn't afford to eat out in the fabulous restaurants or go on the usual tours, but I could afford to go to a cafe and sit for hours and hours and watch the world go by. And during my Zen practice of sitting and watching, I found the world opening up to me in a most delicious way. I learned about fashion, drama, romance, and people. I realized that each person or couple that came into the cafe and sat and smoked a few cigarettes (this was in the days before the smoking bans) played out a kind of miniature drama. There was always a beginning, a middle, and an end. There was a climactic moment. An Aristotelian arc. The couple I spied on was not there simply for the coffee, but for the experience of being out in the world and being a part of the city's passing parade.

I love the fact that the French are completely unabashed about the notion of watching and being watched. In fact, most of the chairs in the outdoor cafes face out to the sidewalk and street. So, even if you are there at a table with a friend, the two of you are still facing out to the world. As a young woman, I let the beauty and intrigue of the city wash over me. I drew pictures and took notes. (Crazy as it sounds, I did not take many photos. I thought that would mark me as a tourist—silly girl!) Still, I was transformed by the experience. And it all came from my little cup of café au lait. Oh, and in terms of pleasure/time/cost analysis, it cost practically nothing. And then later, when I was on the street, passing a cafe, I could do the same—watch the people sitting in the cafe, watching me. I know on the surface, this might seem rather narcissistic or at the very least not very Zen—watching and being watched—but I would like to propose that it is very Zen. The act of watching gets you out of your own way, so that the ego loses some of its grip. For the time you are watching another person, you are traveling in their footsteps and trying on their life and what it would be like to be them. There's great humanity in this. And at the same time, the knowledge that you, too, are being watched helps you develop a certain mindfulness, awareness and focus that requires discipline. You must be present.

Cafe Society

It's true, even today. The French (and many Europeans) still sit in the cafe for hours. This is made possible by waiters who never suggest you've been occupying a particular table long enough and now it's time for you leave and free up a table. They won't even bring your check unless you explicitly ask for it—perhaps a couple of times. Oh, and they'll never look at your half-eaten plate of spinach salad and demand to know whether you're "still working on that?"

And this is true not just in the big cities of Paris, Toulouse, Bordeaux, for instance, but also in the smaller towns and villages. Cafe life is an important part of the culture and, dare I say, a *sacred* part of the culture. Frenchwomen know that by keeping their Secret Garden they are energized and fortified to take that sense of confidence and joy out in the world. They'll turn off the computer and walk away from it. They are not tethered to their cell phone and answering text messages every few seconds. And so, sitting in a cafe can be either a part of their Secret Garden—a place they visit to be alone with their thoughts—or it can be a very social place where they meet up with friends to talk and laugh and flirt.

Café Americain

As an American, you can find Zen in a cup of coffee (or tea, for that matter). And you can discover it at your own local coffee shop, or Starbucks or Peets or Coffee Bean & Tea Leaf. Start by asking for a real cup! Sit in a place where you can watch the world go by. Meet your friends. Starbucks and other cafes now actually encourage you to spend some time in the shop. They've made their cafes cozy and often have free newspapers and books and games and cushy chairs.

Some have little fireplaces and most have big windows facing the street and little cafe tables set up outdoors. Many have bulletin boards with local news and information and my cafe features local artists' work that changes every month and hosts a little gallery party to celebrate the current artist. It's true, coffee isn't as cheap as it once was, so why not get all you can out of the cost of that coffee and stay a while?

You Have a Choice

Everything you do in life has the potential to add to your happiness, your *joie de vivre.* You can grab a cup of coffee and take it out and drink it while you're driving or walking down the street, talking on your cell phone and not really paying any attention to the world around you, and not really enjoying your cup of coffee, or you can buy your coffee, sit down, and drink it from a real china cup. Find a great place to sit where you have a good view of passersby. Rather than multitasking, why not be present to the moment and do one thing at a time?

And here's a radical thought: consider doing nothing. Absolutely nothing.

Still, the truth is, you're never doing "nothing." Even if you're sitting in a cafe and not drinking your latte, you are still doing something. You are observing your world. You are watching people go by. You decide you must find a pair of red vintage cowboy boots, or suddenly make the decision to never get a facelift. Then again, perhaps you find yourself falling in love with a funny-looking man in a pork pie hat. Or you decide that lady crossing the street reminds you of your mother and you are reminded of how much you miss her.

You see, this simple act of sitting and watching can fill you up, inspire you, and give you new ideas, fashion tips, connect you to the past and the present. And the cafe can actually become your own Secret Garden.

In America, we've come to think that bigger and faster is better. But suppose it's the opposite—smaller and slower is better?

That's Zen.

Is Your Refrigerator Running?

When I was growing up, we liked to play this joke: We would call up a neighbor and ask—in a very official Sears Roebuck kind of voice, "Excuse me, ma'am, is your refrigerator running?" If the neighbor hadn't already had this joke played on her, she would answer, "Why yes, it's running just fine." And then we would say, "Well, then you better go chase it!" And then we'd have to hang up because we were doubled over, laughing hysterically. We thought this was the height of comedy.

But in France, this joke is impossible, because French appliances don't *run*, they "walk." In France, you might say, *"ça ne marche pas,"* meaning it's not working (but literally translated it means "it's not walking"). And appliances aren't "working," either. They are walking or not walking. Well, *marche* or *ça ne marche pas*, but you get the idea. Even in the context of simple everyday expressions, we see the French penchant for slowing down a bit, taking their time. Even their appliances are taking their time and walking.

Certainly, Frenchwomen walk everywhere. It's a way of staying toned, but also a way to stay grounded and connected to the earth beneath them. It's a way to commune with nature and connect to friends and neighbors in the community. I cannot help but think that the fact that one's refrigerator walks rather than runs must affect the way a Frenchwoman (or man) thinks about food, meals, electricity, and the passage of time.

Elegance Every Day

My French tutor Marceline has never told me her age. It's just not very French to reveal one's age. Our appointments are made on a strictly week-by-week basis. When I give Marceline a little gift, she will send me a very pretty thank-you card by old-fashioned post. In fact, the other day I received a little card from her in the mail with a photograph of two wooly lambs (she says I'm her lamb) and a little pressed wildflower. I treasure her letters and cards!

She doesn't do e-mail. She doesn't use the computer. She likes to read poetry and novels and watch old black-and-white movies on the Turner Classics Network. And yes, she lives a life of Zen. When I visit, there is always a new flower or fruit arrangement on her dining room table where we work. During the spring, she might have some fragrant hyacinths and during the winter, a little bowl of clementines. She serves mineral water on a tray. Always with a delicate slice of lemon or lime. The tray is part of the charm. Two simple glasses of water can suddenly seem so festive, even ceremonial, when placed on a tray with pretty napkins and a pair of coasters.

When I first met Marceline she told me I would be a good student because I am very curious. She told me that this is the secret to life. And later, gradually, she has revealed the story of her childhood in France and how she appreciates everything—from the little glasses of mineral water, to her flowers in the garden and her collection of hand-written letters and photographs.

Marceline takes nothing for granted, and I must admit that I've learned a whole lot more than how to speak French from her. Marceline teaches me about how to live life well. And truth be told, she reminds me more than a little of my grandmother. Marceline always looks elegant when I arrive. She is very slender and always wears just a touch of pink lipstick and always a beautiful scarf and some pretty jewelry. She wears one of the Guerlain perfumes, but in true Frenchwoman fashion, she will not reveal the name of her particular perfume. This will remain a mystery. Oh, and her hair? Always in an upswept little chignon atop her head.

I know that Marceline practices the ancient art of feng shui, a kind of Zen meditation, on a daily basis. Feng shui is the practice of arranging objects in space. Through this careful, conscious arrangement, one honors the past, the present, and the future. One can bring creativity, beauty, and power into one's life by being aware of the secret language of color, form, direction, and attention to detail. Certainly, these two shimmering glasses of mineral water, with a single sliver of lemon floating on top, placed carefully on a colorful tray, sitting on the table with freshly cut flowers from her very own garden, is essential feng shui. And a French lesson with Marceline is a lesson in Zen. I must let go of preconceived ideas of learning to *Speak French in Ten Easy Steps!*, and rather learn a Jacque Prévert poem or how to pick daisy petals in French to find out if my love loves me back. Rather than reciting, "He loves me, he loves me not," Marceline has me pluck the petals and recite after her:

> *Il m'aime un peu.* (He loves me a little.)
> *Beaucoup.* (A lot.)
> *Passionnément.* (Passionately.)
> *À la folie.* (Madly.)
> *Pas du tout.* (Not at all.)

DON'T YOU JUST love how this is so much more complicated than the simple "He love me, he loves me not"? There is lots of room for the many stages of love and romance and possibility for the heart to change at any moment. When love is like this, you can't help but be present. Zen.

There's Nothing to Do but Eat and Drink and Walk

Last year, I woke up in a hotel in Toulouse on a Sunday morning. The young lady at the front desk informed me that since it was Sunday most of the shops were closed and there was nothing to do but "eat and drink and walk." And so this is what I did. Later that afternoon, while sitting in the Place du Capitole I met a lovely university student named Jasmine. We got into a conversation and she told me how she is studying graphic design and dreams of coming to America one day. We talked for almost an hour and then it was time for her to go home, but she said she'd love to meet up with me later. Now, here's the funny thing—my first impulse was to say oh, no, I'm too busy. But I wasn't too busy. After all, it was Sunday and all I had to do was walk and eat and drink. Still, it was interesting to me that my first impulse was to say I'm busy. And yet, I wasn't busy at all and I realized this was just my automatic American response and I needed to slow down.

And so, we agreed to meet later that evening for a *bière avec grenadine.* This is a delicious drink made up of beer with grenadine syrup. It's also turns the beer a pretty ruby red color and adds a sweetness. (As a side note, you can make your own grenadine by combining an equal amount of pomegranate juice to sugar and shaking well until the sugar is dissolved and then refrigerating. Grenadine is also a key ingredient to making Shirley Temples—my drink of choice as a child!)

Jasmine and I spent a terrific evening together in the cool part of town, away from all the tourists, and while I initially felt strange to be out with a girl who was my daughter's age, I soon relaxed and found that we had a lot in common and that I had a lot to learn from this very intelligent (and beautiful!) young lady. When we talked about *joie de vivre,* she told me how important it is for a person to take their time. She told me that she envisions American women as rushing about all the time. And then she described how it is important to find your equilibrium and she said, "*C'est Zen, non?*" And I said, Yes, that's Zen. And very French.

Get a Little Fresh

Once back in Auvillar I joined Denise and Cheryl on the weekly market trip to Valence d'Agen. This is how I learned about the French way to buy produce. Later that afternoon, Denise Emanuel Clemen, the American writer from Los Angeles, told me how she had asked the man at the fruit stand for a bag of pears and he asked her when she would be eating them. She asked why. And he told her he could give her a pear that was ripe now and she could eat today, and one that would be ripe by tomorrow, and another that would ripen in three days. And then he proceeded to carefully and lovingly pick out the perfect pears for her and put them in a little brown bag. Later, when we enjoyed this pear with our dinner, you can be sure we appreciated it because it was at its peak of ripeness and lovingly chosen for us.

Frenchwomen know about the fleeting nature of life and freshness. They buy their bread every day and for them, this is not an inconvenience, but an opportunity to take a little walk, get out in the fresh air, meet up with neighbors and friends, to chat with their local *boulangerie* proprietor. Nobody hoards a dozen loaves of bread in their freezer. Very few French people buy in bulk. I'm sure part of this comes from their deep-seated philosophy that you never know what tomorrow might bring. Another invasion? In any event, they feel it's not wise to plan too far into the future.

As Americans, we probably think we're saving money by buying in bulk, but in order to store that thirty pounds of beef, we end up actually spending more to get the extra freezer and haul it into our already crowded garage. And then there's the extra electricity to consider. That gets expensive, too. It's hard to believe that a defrosted whatever is as delicious as the one you bought that day at your butcher. And you lose an opportunity for happiness, for connecting with other people and socializing, when you buy in bulk at an anonymous superstore. How can you build a community this way? How can you find balance? How can you connect to your heart center? Honestly, the superstore is not Zen and it is certainly not French and it definitely won't bring you happiness. (Yes, there are plenty of very big stores in France and there is the *supermarché*, but you won't see anything as gigantic as Walmart.)

Good news: Even Walmart has woken up to the news that bigger is not necessarily better. I am happy to report that the megachain has been quietly experimenting with a new kind of shopping experience for the hinterlands. Rather than one enormous, anonymous box, they have built a series of smaller stores, called "Marketside," in Arizona. These small shops actually strive to replicate a village, with a little bakery, a deli, and a fresh produce stand as well as a cafe area. American women have spoken and our big corporations are beginning to listen!

Even if you live in a place where there is only one enormous supermarket, it is still possible to get to know your butcher or the fish man (or woman) and to make a real connection. I often ask my Stop and Shop fish man for advice on cooking a particular fish and he is more than happy to help. This is also a wonderful way for a woman to practice her flirting. Don't get me wrong, I'm a married lady, but it's important to take every opportunity to practice the fine art of conversation and of course to see and be seen.

Even at the fish department of the Stop and Shop!

Learning the Art of the French Shrug

One day, Marceline told me that if I want to learn French, the first thing I need to learn is to shrug. Then she demonstrated the French shrug to me. It's a very powerful little gesture. You purse your lips, perhaps puff them out slightly, then you raise your shoulders, turn your head. Oh, and if you really want to go all the way, you can roll your eyes and look heavenward, as if to say only God really knows and you might add, "*C'est comme ça!*" (That's the way it is!)

This has been a very powerful little lesson for me. I'm the type of gal who often apologizes for no reason at all. I will often say "I'm sorry" to people as a kind of prophylactic measure, just to cover all my bases and in case I did do something wrong in the past, the present, or even if I'm about to do something bad in the next fifteen minutes. Please don't think I'm completely weird. I know other women who have this habit of apologizing for no reason.

Not too long ago, my husband pointed out my habit of saying "I'm sorry" all the time, and suggested that I should come up with a phrase that's a little less self-deprecating and more empowering. And so, after much thought, I came up with my substitute phrase for "I'm sorry." My substitute phrase for "I'm sorry" would be "*C'est la vie.*" That's life. I decided I would say this, along with the French shrug.

But since this habit of apologizing has been with me for a long time, I didn't have a lot of faith in the power of my resolution. Then, one night, I had an opportunity to try it out. My husband and I were watching TV together and there was a commercial break, during which the volume suddenly increased. You know how they do that—to get your attention and to get you to buy some yogurt that will help out your digestive tract or ask your doctor about a prescription for some antianxiety medication. My husband turned to me and said in a slightly accusing voice, "Aren't you going to lower the volume?" I turned to him, a little confused. After all, he had possession of the remote. He continued. "Can't you hear how loud that is?"

Now, my first reaction was to quickly say, "I'm sorry!" And then ask for the remote and lower the volume. But instead, I just shrugged. The truth is I hadn't really noticed that big a difference in the volume. And so, I added, *"C'est la vie."*

Well, this really took him aback. But you know what? He lowered the volume and didn't say another word and I felt somehow much stronger.

Now I'm not suggesting that we stop apologizing when there's really something to apologize for, but I am suggesting that it might be a good idea to simply let a few things slide. After all, you are not responsible for the health and well-being of the entire world! Learn to say *c'est la vie!* Learn the power of the shrug!

Date Night

When you've been married for a while, it's easy to get into a routine. Actually, more than a routine, it's easy to get into a rut. I know from personal experience that this can happen and while Frenchwomen have a certain advantage over us in that they are often invited out to dinner parties, we can still make sure that we, too, add some new experiences into our romantic relationships. Begin by hosting a few dinner parties. This way, you'll soon be invited to your friends' homes for dinner parties. In addition to this, why not create a "date night"—a night that you set aside for just you and your husband or partner? By making space in your life for just the two of you, you will find that after a time you become more and more creative about what you'll do for your date night. This doesn't have to mean you'll go out to a Broadway show and an expensive dinner. Your date night could mean a picnic in the park at sunset or a walk in your neighborhood. It could be a game of miniature golf or just setting time aside to listen to music and play cards. My husband and I will often spend a cold winter's night playing gin rummy by the wood-burning stove. You might think this sounds boring, but if you try it, I guarantee that you will find it surprisingly sexy. Yes, sexy. Much sexier than watching a *Law & Order* rerun on the TV!

Live in the Moment

Frenchwomen know that when you take care to appreciate the little things in one's life—the details, the simplest pleasures, and the smallest gestures—you need less in the way of material goods. When you truly take your time to enjoy sitting in a cafe and enjoy your coffee slowly, you don't need a supersized cup to place in your car's cup holder to drink while driving sixty miles an hour to your next appointment. You don't need five loaves of bread when you have one delicious artisan baguette that you bought from your very own neighborhood baker. You don't need ten pairs of jeans when you've found the one pair that fits you perfectly. You don't need that impossibly expensive necklace when you have your grandmother's pearls. You don't need to buy new dishes in that up-to-the-minute design when you appreciate and use your good china on a daily basis. You don't go overboard, exhausting yourself over the holidays when you make every day an occasion for friendship and family, fun and celebration.

If happiness is an experience that we share, then shopping in bulk at a big-box store—where we never get to know the shop owner, the butcher, or the fish man, the girl who sells the muffins—will never bring us happiness. If we only do something once a month or so and we don't interact with people, we are not sharing the experience. If our entire family microwaves and cooks individual meals at different, separate times, we miss out on one of the great joys of life.

And even if you're making a microwave dinner, you can still eat together and serve each meal on a real plate and sit down together as a family. It's about the experience of the shared dinner, the conversation, and taking your time.

Truthfully, it is completely possible to bring a little Zen *à la française* into our busy American lives. Perhaps we can't sit in a cafe for three hours, but consider finding the time on a Saturday to sit and watch and daydream for one hour. Practice the fine art of mindfulness by simply paying closer attention to your posture, the way you walk, your presence in the world. Are you kind to people? Do you listen? Part of the reason why I suggest that we frequent smaller shops in our own communities is this will lead to knowing and caring about our neighbors. You are part of something bigger than yourself and when you get into conversations, you learn that we are all connected and the world is, indeed, a very small place. It's also a very big place.

French Lessons

TAKE THIS WEEK and practice the art of "less is more." Rather than doing one big trip to the supermarket, buy only what you need each day. It may sound like a lot of work at first, but you'll see that it's actually much easier to select a few items that you'll have for dinner that night. It also will help you with portion control and to truly appreciate fresh food.

Next, take a look at your closets. Is there something—say, a gorgeous velvet scarf—that you've been saving for that special occasion but the time never seemed right? The time is now. Put it on now and enjoy it. On the other hand, if you've got boxes of old clothes or gifts that you really don't like, give them away! Make room for something beautiful to come into your life.

Arrange for a "date night" with your husband or partner. It's an opportunity to connect with your original premarriage selves and a great way to reignite your romance.

Find a local cafe or coffee shop and make it your own. Observe your world and get into conversations with people. Learn to be a good listener. You are an important presence in your world. Whether you realize it or not, you are an inspiration and make a difference. Stand up straight. Smile. Dress well. Be kind. People are watching.

Be in the moment and be willing to change your plans when something unique and wonderful comes into your life. If you don't overbook and overextend yourself, this should be easier to do. Follow Marceline's lead, and practice the art of arrangement. Little touches like placing fresh flowers or a bowl of fruit on your dining room table or putting a fresh flower in your hair are simple to do and add a whole lot of *joie de vivre* to your life and the lives of those around you.

And finally, learn to occasionally just shrug your shoulders and say, "That's life!"

CHAPTER SIX

En Plein Air

(In the Fullness of the Outdoors)

Let us be grateful to people who make us happy, they are the charming gardeners who make our souls blossom.

—MARCEL PROUST

IT HAD RAINED the night before and now the sun has come out, leaving the vineyards of Southern France a brilliant green. The grape leaves are damp and heavy with the weight of rainwater and the grapes are covered with droplets of dew.

The grapes at Domaine de Thermes are nothing like the ones I'm used to buying at the Stop and Shop. These grapes are darkly purple, small, and bunched tightly together, nestled under the leaves as if too shy to be seen in the morning sunlight.

Dominique Jollet Péraldi and Thierry Combarel are the owners of the winery that makes Côtes du Brûlhois wine from these grapes. They're a young couple, with tons of energy and impossibly good-looking. In addition to the Côtes du Brûlhois, they also produce a delicious rosé (made from the merlot and côt). We've been enjoying that rosé quite a lot during the hot summer days at the colony. Oh, and they also produce Cuvée Dothi, a very dark, very delicious, almost black wine. Yum.

The sun is fully out now and here we are—the little group from the Virginia Center for the Arts in Auvillar, Denise, John, and me—along with fifteen or twenty people from the village of Auvillar and the neighboring villages. There are men and women of all ages. There is a couple that must be in their sixties, there's a very pretty *femme*, who I think might be married to the man who is here to pick grapes. There is a little family of three—a mother, father, and their beautiful teenage daughter, Manon.

Manon of the Spring

Manon speaks almost perfect English and she is able to explain to me that her family is actually Dutch, but they live here in a village called Lauzerte. She's seventeen years old, almost eighteen. She's tall and slender and has the most sparkling green eyes imaginable and beautiful blonde hair, so she doesn't look like a typical French girl. Perhaps it was her exotic looks that captivated the vineyard owners' teenage son, because soon after the two sets of parents met, these two young people fell in love.

There's a festivity to this day in the vineyard. Excitement is in the air and a sense of anticipation for a day of fun. We jump onto the back of the vineyard's truck and then we're driven to a row of grapevines. We are taken for a rather bumpy ride up and down and then up again to the top of the line of grapes, where we jump off the truck and are soon handed big plastic buckets and pairs of bright orange shears. As we find our place along the rows of vines, the vineyard owner's golden retriever follows us around, running up and down the sloping hills, sniffing occasionally as if checking in on our progress. We work fast, clipping off the bunches of grapes and placing them in the buckets, moving down the rows until we get to the end, where we dump our buckets filled with grapes into the back of another truck and hop on board the smaller truck, which takes us to another part of the vineyard. And so the day goes.

The atmosphere is friendly and festive and, indeed, we have a little party on the patio when we are all done and after the grapes have been put through a funny-looking red machine that separates the stems from the fruit and another machine that washes the grapes in a giant vat.

It is later at the party on the patio where we enjoy some wine and cheese and bread that I have a chance to talk to Manon and her mother. Manon tells me about what *joie de vivre* means to her. She loves the country life. Later, she will send this in an e-mail to me:

> I love being with my friends, walking in the forest, swimming in our lake, reading in our garden, sitting in the sun. But there's also the French "ambience" which makes us feel fine. I'm a very sociable person. I grew up in the country, far from every human being. My village is called Lauzerte, which is in the southwest of France, next to Toulouse. My house is made of wonderful white stones, which are

> a specialty of the houses here. I have three brothers and one sister, so I was like a boy when I was a little girl. I loved playing outside in the fields, and I swam in a lake. . . . In June, I'm going to have my end exam, the baccalaureat, which is necessary to go to the university. Next year, I'll study English, to become a teacher later or an interpreter.

And from Manon's mother:

> Country life is really fantastic! There's nothing in town which can attract me. Above all, I'm proud of the life that my children can have in the French country, I think that it's better for their growing up. The wild life in the nature! My greatest pleasure is the fact that I can read a book before I fall asleep without any stress. And when I'm with my husband and my children, around a table. But I like also having an "apéro" with some friends, of course drinking wine coming from "Thermes"! It's also something special to do the "vendanges" [community grape harvesting].

Green Acres

I will let you in on a secret. I'm not a big nature girl. And so, it's amazing and perhaps even a little intimidating when I hear the Frenchwomen speak so poetically of their love of the countryside. In France, even city girls love their farms and fields. And you will find that a Parisian woman will spend her weekends visiting her parents' home outside the city—often in the South or up north in Normandy, by the seashore. When my Parisian friend Sylvie visits her parents' home in

Vézalay, she brings back homemade jams that her mother made from their fruit trees.

But still, if you live in a big city in America and feel you have no access to the country, you can still enjoy fresh food and the joys of gardening and harvesting. My dear friend Mary Kelly always finds ways to incorporate nature into her life as a New Yorker. She has a passion for cooking and even grows flowers on her fire escape. This is what she recently told me about how she enjoys the "rural" delights of living in a big city:

> New York City is filled with wonderful, exotic food markets offering all things imaginable, for a price, from the four corners of the world. Yet what has become one of my greatest delights, as a dweller of this fine city, is the Union Square farmers' market. Here, four days every week, farmers, artisans, and fishermen come to entice me with their produce, cheese, eggs, bread, organic meats and poultry, seafood, even wine and honey; all grown, raised, produced, or caught within two hundred miles of my humble studio apartment. At tented tables on the northern edge of Union Square I have discovered and fallen in love with things I've never known before—ramps, garlic scapes, tiny La Ratte potatoes, and a variety of apple called honeycrisp. Shopping the farmers' market is the simplest way to bring sweet, delicious joy to my urban world.
>
> But I have also found a way to play farmer myself, by joining a community garden on West 104th Street. Although I live downtown in Chelsea, a mere nine stops north on the subway, I tend a plot just

four feet by eight that may be humble in size, but magnificent in ambition. I grow tomatoes; Cherokee purples, striped Germans, Eva purple balls, and Tiny Tims. I grow hot peppers; jalapeños, serranos, and red cherries. I sneak lettuces between the bigger plants; arugula, red leaf, romaine, buttercrunch, and mizuna. Herbs hang off the edges; I grow basil, thyme, rosemary, oregano, parsley, mint, and one very large shrub of sage. This is my own small piece of heaven. Eating a tomato that I have nurtured and grown on the island of Manhattan is a thrill I cannot fully describe.

Town and Country

It doesn't really matter where you live. You can also enjoy both the city and the country. If you live in the country already, or even the suburbs, why not really take advantage of your good fortune and plant a vegetable garden this spring? Spend time walking in the fresh air. Buy a bicycle and rediscover the joys of racing in the wind. And if you live in a city, then look into shared city gardens or a neighborhood community that wants to beautify your block by planting flowers and protecting your local trees. My good friend Laurie Graff, a terrific writer and an actress, lives on New York City's Upper West Side. She's a perfect example of a city girl who enjoys being *en plein air* as much as possible. During the summers, you will find her running through Central Park and at the first snow, she gets out her cross-country skis and off she goes through the winter wonderland. Once, there was a blizzard and Amsterdam Avenue was completely closed down and she actually skied down the street. And she wasn't alone. Lots of New Yorkers do this!

You see, a trip to the country doesn't have to be a big expensive vacation. Consider short weekend getaways with friends where you pick apples or help out on an organic farm. You don't have to be a total country girl to enjoy the country. In fact, I'll never forget the day I was about to leave for Boston when my husband, who was fishing at the end of the dock, called me over and asked me to cast a reel or two. Well, even though I was all dressed up, I cast one reel and *voilà*! I actually caught a striped bass wearing lipstick and high heels—me that is, not the fish!

My husband is quite the fisherman and gardener, too, and I will tell you the truth, I don't think I would have ever come to the country if it weren't for him. But I am glad I did. I am happy to have this challenge in my life. I am happy to learn something new. I am happy that I'm actually able to surprise myself at this stage of my life! People who've known me for years as the red-lipstick girly girl were shocked when I sent them a photo of me with my big striped bass. And to be perfectly honest, that was probably half the fun for me!

And in all seriousness, I am happy to be able to go out in the garden and pick fresh basil. I am thrilled to bite into a garden-grown, sunshine-infused ruby red tomato. And I am more than happy to get my hands a little dirty and dig for those potatoes at the bottom of the earth.

Panties on the Line

When I first learned that there was no clothes dryer at Virginia Center for the Creative Arts in Auvillar, I must admit I was a little distressed. Yes, there was a clothesline out there in the field, but I hadn't washed and hung clothes on a line since I was a little girl and even then, I'm not sure how often I did it. I will say this, I said a silent thank-you that my panties were very pretty and lacey and nothing to be embarrassed about. In fact, I was a little proud of them. Yes, I will admit that when the day came to do my first laundry, I was kind of thrilled to be hanging my delicates on a line to dry in the sunny field.

Actually, I arranged my laundry for optimum visual appeal. All the white panties together, then the black panties, then the nighties—all floating gauzy and sheer and lacey in the warm autumn breeze. To the side, I clothes-pinned the skirts and tops and the one pair of jeans I had brought with me. The panties took center stage.

I stood back and was very pleased with myself. This was fun and I enjoyed the little upper-arm workout. There was something so lovely and old-fashioned and poignant about hanging up my laundry and my panties looked so pretty that I appreciated good lingerie in a whole new way.

The Right to Dry

All this may sound very trivial and more than a little silly, but I really think hanging up your own laundry occasionally can make a big difference in your life. First of all, when you see your laundry like that—right out there in the brightness of the midday sun—well, you might consider replacing those old panties or the dingy sheets with the stain in the middle. Plus, using your dryer a little less can make a big difference to our use of natural resources. There's actually a group called the Right to Dry Movement that supports the individual's right to hang clothes on a clothesline. Apparently, this is controversial in a few places. But think about it. If we hung our clothes out to dry even a few times a year, wouldn't we make an impact? And it's such a simple thing to do. It doesn't cost anything. And afterwards, your clothes smell like sunshine!

Buy Local

Frenchwomen love to shop just as much as American women. Perhaps even more when you consider how often they go out to buy their fresh bread—generally every morning! They love the camaraderie and familiarity that comes from shopping at the same place on a regular basis. They know the shopkeepers and the shopkeepers know them. And at the outdoor markets where they buy their fruits and vegetables, they are more likely to run into their friends and neighbors. Friendships with neighbors are solidified and fortified over years of friendly exchanges over the bins of fresh leeks and bunches of basil. And you'll find these farmers' markets not just in the countryside, but in the big cities, as well. They're all over Paris and the markets don't just sell fresh produce. Often, they sell clothing, costume jewelry, and kitchen gadgets. In fact, I noticed that in several of the markets I went to there was a very entertaining man who demonstrated a little appliance to cut vegetables in all different shapes. He was very theatrical and funny and when he came to cutting up cucumbers into ringlets, he held them up to his ear and joked about how they would make good earrings, too! The crowd roared with laughter, and honestly, I felt so happy to be out there with this group of people on a Saturday morning. I couldn't help but compare this to my usual trek to the Stop and Shop, which—let's be honest—is not the most entertaining place to shop in the world!

But here's the good news—the French do not have a monopoly on the farmers' market. There are lots of them right here in America. Mary Kelly's Union Square farmers' market is a great example. I just learned that Minnesota has formed its own Farmers' Market Association to create a unified voice among their many farmers' markets. Southern California has something called "Farmer's Net." And here in my own little corner of the world, Falmouth, Massachusetts, a few locals have started a farmers' market on Main Street. I often get news about it via e-mails and I've followed the struggle to start and maintain the farmers' market. It grows stronger and more popular every year.

So, you can see, no matter where you live, it is possible to have your own outdoor market. Your own *en plein air* experience.

Here's some advice—the next time you go to your farmers' market, make it special. Wear something festive for the occasion, perhaps a long white linen skirt and a big straw hat. Bring along that vintage basket your mother gave you. And take your time. The farmers' market isn't just about buying a few tomatoes, it's about getting out there in the world and being seen. It's about forming and maintaining friendships. It's about the power of being committed to something in your community, supporting your local farmers, and giving back in the form of being a part of this performance-art installation called life.

Get Cooperative

In Toulouse, my friend Béatrice (she's the one who offered us the great quiche recipe) goes to a farm cooperative and she picks up her fresh vegetables every week. They're all ready and waiting for her in a lovely basket when she arrives at the coop each Friday afternoon. She signed up at the beginning of the season, paid her fee, and then the vegetables are there and waiting for her to pick up each week.

I imagined that this was something you could only do in France, until I got home and began going on and on to my local friends about the great farm cooperative and how Béatrice gets her basket of delicious vegetables every Friday. And then my neighbors told me that there was such a program right here in my own backyard. Yes, we have Coonamessett Farm, a twenty-acre farming and research enterprise that not only provides fresh produce, but also has summer buffets with reggae music! Sometimes you have to leave home and travel to find that you have some wonderful and magical things right in your own backyard and that there really is no place like home. And while it's so much fun to grow and harvest your own vegetables, if you can't do this, there is still a way to find fresh food. Oh, there's an iPhone app to help find your local farmers' market—so no excuses!

Sunday in the Park

How do Frenchwomen find and keep their *joie de vivre*? Well, every Frenchwoman is an individual, just as every American woman is an individual. But when I asked Béatrice about my search for *joie de vivre*, she suggested if I wanted to find a good example, I must go to a particular park with a carousel in the center of Toulouse. What a discovery! This little park was filled with children playing, teenagers flirting, *grand-mères* and *grandpères* watching the young ones. Lots of friends chatting and laughing. I particularly enjoyed watching a couple in their late sixties, sitting close together on a park bench and holding hands. This day in the park was pure theater! Everyone was dressed beautifully, artfully. It was so obvious from this afternoon adventure that the French love to watch and be watched.

More than this, the park revealed a joy in nature, in walking and in beautiful gardens and sculpture. And yes, lots of voluptuous naked women—the statues, that is. I was amazed how such simple things could bring so much delight.

This day in the park should be easy for any American woman to emulate. It's simply a matter of getting together with a few friends, choosing a bench in a local park in your town square, and agreeing to meet there on a regular basis. Before you know it, others will get the idea and you'll create your own little "French park" in your own hometown. Oh, and if you live in a cold climate, find a cafe, a coffee shop, or a library with a social room. It doesn't have to be a fancy place—I often run into my friends at our local Starbucks in Falmouth. True, it's not quite as nice at the Café de Flore in Paris, but when I run into so many people in the town that I know and love, well, even Starbucks is transformed into something quite magical!

Oh, Joy—It's Raining Cats and Dogs!

The French love their pets. They bring them everywhere. You'll see cats running underfoot in restaurants. You'll see dogs at outdoor concerts and sitting beside their mistresses in cafes, waiting patiently as she sips her espresso and reads her book.

But here's what I found interesting about the French. They don't seem to have this division between being a dog person or a cat person. I've often met people who have a dog and they say they hate cats and that cats are mischievous and can't be trusted. Then I meet a cat person and they'll say, oh, they don't like dogs because dogs are too outgoing, too slobbery. And I can't help but think, they're really talking about something deeper, something Freudian perhaps, and that all this division in the animal kingdom is really about dividing men and women.

In America, we often have our guys' night out and our girls' night out, but in France—the Frenchwomen tell me—they love to mix it up! They see no point in having a party if there isn't that delicious tension and attention from the opposite sex. Oh, and they don't actually have this expression—"the opposite sex"—in France.

And I'm amazed to see, it's the same with cats and dogs! They love them both!

Bonnie the Cat

One day, I was working in my studio in Auvillar and I looked out the window and saw our neighbor walking her collie dog. She's *une femme d'un certain âge* and I would often see her coming and going down the street. But this particular day, she stopped in front of our gate to pet Bonnie, our neighbor Lucy's calico cat. This lady spent quite a bit of time talking to Bonnie, while her collie dog stood by patiently.

Her dog did not bark or fuss and I had to assume this was because he was used to his mistress befriending cats, as well as dogs. For me, it was lovely to spy on this lady cooing and scratching Bonnie's neck as she purred and the collie seemed to communicate in his own way.

It seems to me that when we get into the either you're a cat person or a dog person mentality, we lose some of our sense of balance and *joie de vivre.* It reveals a way of thinking that is not always good for us. The French are able to live in the middle ground, because they don't go overboard in either direction. They are able to eat wonderful food and not gain weight, because they are not into the idea of feast or famine. They are into pleasure. They are not wearing lingerie because they're in love or wearing sweats because they are out of love, but rather they are a little sexy all the time. And no, they are not dog people or cat people. They love both, because they love life . . . all in proper balance!

My friend and sister Francophile Tracey Cleantis, who writes a blog for *Psychology Today,* recently adopted a little dog and named her Lily. When I asked her to tell me about the experience—oh, and by the way, up until this point she had only had cats—this is what she wrote:

Bonjour, Lily!

> I had always wanted a dog. I would, when people asked, describe myself as a dog person—even though I'd never had one before. I had always imagined, since childhood, that my first dog would be a black Labrador named Jake who would wear a red bandanna. But when I started actually looking for

my first dog, it turned out that it was to be a West Highland white terrier named Lily.

When I met Lily for the first time I felt what the Grinch reportedly felt after hearing the Whos in Whoville sing their Christmas song: my heart grew nine times bigger. There isn't a day that goes by that I don't find myself loving her more than I imagined possible. My Lily, I know, has expanded my capacity for love. This "Westie who's the bestie" melts my heart. You see, my heart had been broken by infertility treatment that failed to lead to the birth of a baby. With each failed round of IVF my heart broke a little more and I felt sure that it would never be whole again. But when Lily looks up at me with her white fluffiness, her Milk Dud nose, and her beautiful brown eyes, my heart is melted. With that melting she has, by just being her, healed my broken heart.

Lily has taught me so much, as she is incredibly intelligent (we are considering applying to Harvard, where she will undoubtedly do a dual major and graduate with honors). My lovely Lily has taught me the value of healthy narcissism (my dog-daughter has no small measure of self-esteem). She is an extreme extrovert and that has taught this somewhat shy introvert to stop and say hello to every neighbor we meet. Most importantly my gorgeous girl has taught me what unconditional love really looks like. For me, on a hard day, when I feel that happiness has said *au revoir* to me, it would be very easy, if I was on my own, to talk myself out of leaving the house. But then Lily jumps on my bed and greets me with her

> excited, waggly-tailed, happy hello-world face—and I have to leave my ennui at the door and grab her leash and say "*Bonjour*, Lily. *Bonjour*, happiness!"

How funny and how delightful. But I also found Tracey's story particularly moving because a few months before my trip to Paris, my beloved orange tabby, Sugar, died suddenly. He was twelve years old, but still, I was heartbroken, so much so that every time I went to the animal rescue shelter, I spent much of the time telling them about Sugar and what a wonderful cat he was, and then I would often pick up a kitten or two and then leave in tears. Clearly, I was not ready to adopt a new cat. However, after my last stay in Auvillar and meeting Bonnie, Lucy's calico, and also Béatrice's orange tabby, something in me changed.

Bonjour, Mom! *Bonjour*, Dad!

Say your parents live in the sticks. In the suburbs. In the country. Let's say they still live in that house where you grew up. It's very uncool. Rather than just tolerating this time away from your friends and the city and all that hustle and bustle, consider this a kind of Secret Garden. And consider planting a real garden. If we rethink our parents' home and try to make peace with the past, we might find that this place that was once our home is a kind of wellspring for us. There are memories nestled within the blades of grass. There are secrets in the trees. Nature offers us a kind of timelessness that connects us to the past and the future. Even if your parents don't live in the house where you grew up, there is magic to be found in a visit. There are new discoveries to make. And this is especially true as we grow older and find that we can reintroduce ourselves to our parents as friends and let go of some of the long-ago wounds from our childhood. I grew up not really knowing my father. In 1997, we began a cautious and very tenuous friendship. It hasn't always been easy to talk to my father. There was a lot of distance to cover, but I will tell you this—when we walk through his backyard and we look at his garden, and wander around the trees, our conversations flow. Aristotle was known for the habit of walking with his students while talking about science and philosophy. They were called the Peripatetics. Sometimes I think this is what my father and I do. He has a very big backyard and in the springtime the grass is tall and very, very green. The trees are enormous—the size you'd see in a forest—and we have a great time, just strolling around the lawn. There is a compost pile of leaves and coffee grounds. There is a "fort" he built out of large rocks he unearthed. I think he was hoping for grandchildren to come and play there, but that never seemed to happen. Maybe one day it will—not grandchildren anymore (they're all grown)—but perhaps great-grandchildren. My father has a little vegetable garden. Always tomatoes. And in the early summer, zillions of lilies of the valley suddenly multiply around the base of the trees and practically take over the entire lawn for a week or two. And then, just as suddenly, they are gone.

Here's my advice. If you want to get to know your mom or dad, start in the backyard. Start by taking a walk. Fresh air is an elixir and it's the essence of happiness.

French Lessons

FIND A PUBLIC SQUARE in your own hometown and make it your own. Walk to your local market, even if it means driving to a parking lot and then walking. Create a meeting place in nature. Reclaim your public self by dressing for show.

Open your eyes and notice all the beauty in your world. Get into conversations with your local shopkeepers. Talk to the fish man! Ask his advice on how to cook that halibut.

Be alive to your world. Plant some herbs. Find joy in simple activities. Start a private or a community garden.

Wherever you happen to be, look into the possibility that there's a farmers' market nearby. Most towns now have them and they're a great way to get to know your own hometown or a place you're visiting for the first time.

Whenever you can, shop local and buy local. Look for seasonal fruits and vegetables. This is not only a way to get the freshest food, but also a way to live in the moment and to truly enjoy what is available to you in any given month. For instance, I live on Cape Cod, and I know that the local blueberries are only available around July. I wait for them all year long and then truly enjoy them when the time comes, knowing that this is a fleeting indulgence.

Ask yourself where you might have gone overboard in one direction or another in your life. Try not to define yourself in terms of teams or sides, such as, "I'm a sporty girl" or "I'm the brainy type." Look for ways you can be expansive and generous—to yourself, to others, and to the world at large. Be not a cat person or a dog person, but both!

Oh, and if you can, during the warm weather, dry your panties out of doors!

CHAPTER SEVEN

Good Enough to Eat

À votre santé.
(To your health.)

MY LIFE CHANGED FOREVER on a Sunday afternoon in early 2004. I was sitting at my dining room table in New Haven, Connecticut, and I had picked up *The New York Times.* I turned to the Sunday Styles section and I began to read all about the upcoming release of Mireille Guiliano's seminal book *French Women Don't Get Fat.* It hadn't even been released yet, but I could sense the world shifting under my feet.

According to the article, her book was all about losing weight the Frenchwoman way—meaning, you ate smaller portions because you ate strictly for pleasure. You didn't "diet," but rather you were so satisfied with small portions of incredibly delicious real food—sometimes with *butter and chocolate,* yes! When you ate the Frenchwoman way, you were happy and balanced and you never felt the need to binge on an enormous bag of Tostitos tortilla chips (not that I've ever, ever done that).

I immediately called my local bookstore and asked them to put a copy on reserve for me. I have struggled with my weight for years, and in fact, I have been a Weight Watchers member on and off since I turned fourteen and had a total of five pounds to lose. I finally became a card-carrying "lifetime member" in 1985 and I have been fighting the good fight ever since. It hasn't always been easy.

And so, this book, with its cheeky title—*French Women Don't Get Fat*—and the idea of eating for pleasure and finally making peace with food, sounded like paradise to me. Plus, the part about eating bread and real butter and dark chocolate and drinking wine and champagne and still losing weight—well, that sounded pretty darn good, too!

Before the book even came out and before we even had a chance to read it, my friend Susan Dunigan called me to say she had just returned from Paris and was coming over to visit me. She'd bring a bottle of wine and something to eat. Ah, and you know what she brought—yes, a bottle of French wine and an entire round of brie, with a package of Carr's table water crackers. She was wearing a new Hermès scarf with the Qu'importe le Flacon pattern, and still exuded that *I've just been to Paris!* aura about her. We spoke in broken French as I placed the cheese and bread on a platter and uncorked the wine. Susan knew all about Mireille's book and was just as excited as I was at the prospect of getting a copy, reading it, and learning how to eat for pleasure and still lose weight. We decided we would be French! *Ooh la la!* We cried out in unison, clinking our glasses together with *"à votre santé!"* and then proceeded to drink the entire bottle of wine and eat all the cheese and crackers, plus the big bunch of grapes and the cut-up apples that I had provided for "nutritional balance."

How many Weight Watchers points? Probably one hundred. Maybe two hundred. I'm not sure, but it was definitely over a week's worth of points!

How Do You Like It?

When I finally did read *French Women Don't Get Fat,* I realized I had a lot to learn, most of all about portions! They should be small, but I also needed to learn to completely shift my attitude toward food.

But, still, my struggle was this: When you're a big American gal—as I am—with a big American appetite, how do you accept this idea of small portions? How can you feel satisfied when the response to the question, "How do you like it?" is always "More, more, more!" You see, I'm not just talking about just wanting more food, but wanting more love, more money, more compliments, more attention, more dresses, more shoes—more, more, more! I really wanted to know how Frenchwomen manage to be happy with less. How do they overcome their insecurities? Where did they get that *je ne sais quoi*?

I couldn't ask my French grandmother the question—what was her secret to *joie de vivre* or how did she come by all that *savoir vivre*—because, well, she had passed away many years ago.

As an American, I've viewed food to be about much more than nourishment. It's a form of emotional fuel. It's medicinal. It's a happy pill. It provides comfort—perhaps even a kind of numbing from some unspeakable pain. And sometimes it's even a form of revenge. You see, treated without respect, food can be dangerous stuff. It can nourish you and at the same time, it can destroy you.

Perhaps this is why my French grandmother insisted that the kitchen was completely off limits in between meals. I stayed with her and my grandfather during the summers when my mother was in the hospital for "a rest." I do remember the delicious meals she made. Everything was very flavorful. There were always lots of fresh vegetables from their garden. And yes, she put a little butter on the yellow squash and on the green beans. In true French style, she served everything on little plates and there was always just enough, no more. We learned early on not to ask for seconds. Oh, and she always served dessert and I will certainly never forget the fresh peaches with vanilla ice cream that she made with her very own ice cream maker.

But once the meal was over and the dishes washed, the kitchen was closed and completely off limits. During those hot summer afternoons, if she even found me, lurking around the cupboards, she would tell me I should be outside in the fresh air. Later, when I was in my twenties, I read the Judith Krantz novel *Scruples* and was reminded once again of my grandmother when I read the part where the overweight American girl from Boston goes to Paris to live and her housemother actually locks the refrigerator with a padlock in between meals!

The heroine of the story, Valentine, returns home to America later, completely transformed. She's slim and very sophisticated. She has learned the French method of equilibrium and balance. I suspect some attitudes toward food come from a history of deprivation. There was so much lack over the past years that the French take nothing for granted. I've even heard that escargot and frogs legs were not considered a gourmet treat, but they became a "delicacy" really out of necessity. There just wasn't enough of the usual chicken and fish and beef to eat, and so they had to be inventive. I wonder if perhaps the reason why many French *femmes d'un certain âge* are so careful about gaining weight is it's considered unpatriotic to get too big and that staying slim is a way of honoring the struggles their parents and grandparents endured during the wars. With this kind of history, wouldn't overeating and overindulging make a person feel a little guilty? I would think so.

No Cows Here

It is true, in France "grazing" is frowned upon. Mealtime is very important and something to build up an appetite for. Meals are convivial, festive, and an important time in French life where relationships are formed, family issues deconstructed, flames of love reignited, and the topics of the day discussed. It's an important source of pleasure in the French person's life. Conversation is very important. In fact, the art of conversation is elevated to a bit of an art form and when you have someone at the table that is intelligent and witty, well, this person becomes a highly coveted guest.

The Frenchwoman gets so much from dinner with family and friends. She is able to talk about her day and turn the chaos of a variety of events into an orderly narrative. And we all know that women need to talk. We need to be heard. By sitting down to a proper dinner with perhaps some candles and a little music playing—we can truly learn to associate food with *joie de vivre*, and find happiness while breaking bread.

And because food is so inextricably linked to the group dining experience, there's very little opportunity for secret snacking late at night. First of all, you're full from dinner and second of all, it lasts for hours. More than this, the group dinner experience doesn't simply fill the stomach, but through talk and laughter and time sharing there is plenty of food for the heart. And with a happy heart, there really is less of a chance you will leave the table hankering for something that has been left unsatisfied—that emotional part of your being, your soul, if you will, that searches for a feeling of being loved.

Yes, in this context, you could say that food is love. And to feel loved is to feel happy.

The Desire to Be Seen

Still, this new way of eating and honoring food isn't always easy. There are layers of years where food has been used for medicinal purposes. And I must admit, there are times when I wonder if I have something invested in being overweight. Not in actually being overweight, but sometimes I think I may have something invested in feeling a little bad about myself and feeling *not quite good enough*, almost as if when it comes to beauty and being out in the world, I actually want a little "handicap," almost in the same sense that a golfer gets a handicap, and in this way not too much is expected of me. I know for me, this word "handicap" is quite loaded. My mother was handicapped after we were in a terrible car accident and because I came through it comparatively unscathed, I grew up always feeling a little guilty.

And so, if I did not have this handicap of being overweight, then I sometimes imagine I would be very powerful and strong and confident. But then, if I were powerful and strong and confident—I fear that more would be expected of me, or perhaps that other women wouldn't like me. And so, there's this handicap, this extra weight that tells the world, *See, I'm vulnerable, too.*

You'd think being large would make one feel strong and big, but it doesn't. It is a kind of punishment to yourself. It's like forcing yourself to walk around with your underpants on your head. Something everyone can see: "Hey, she's got underpants on her head. What's wrong with her?!" Perhaps that's part of the equation—I want to be seen—in all my vulnerability. I think that all women with this issue—even a woman I admire very much, like Oprah Winfrey—have a strong need to be accepted and loved for who they are right now, despite or even because of all their struggles with weight. We feel vulnerable and maybe handicapped, but we are here. In all our human fragility and imperfection, we are here.

Real Bodies

Now, if all this is true, then there's some good news. There's a solution, and I believe Frenchwomen can help us with this. If we struggle with weight issues, then we need to be accepted. Right now. In all our imperfection, we need to be seen. Start by walking. Yes, it's back to that! You may not live in Paris or a village in France where you can walk to the market every day, but you can certainly park your car farther away from the store and increase your time walking. If you have a little downtown with shops, try parking at one end, and then walk up and down the street to do your errands. Bring a canvas or a straw shopping bag. Walking is great exercise and just about anyone can do it, plus carrying your groceries is terrific for building upper-arm strength. But more than this, it is a wonderful way to connect your mind to your spirit and to your body. If you're out of shape, you'll soon feel it. You'll get breathless and tired. This is no small thing, because if you're always driving from place to place, it's easy to put on some extra pounds and not really notice it. But when you're walking, you definitely feel it. Plus, you are definitely being seen. You become conscious of other people's reactions to your presence. Do they smile when they see you wearing that beautiful blue scarf? Are they intrigued by your boots? And you can see yourself in the reflection of shop windows. All this helps to build a sense of presence in the world. No, you are not invisible.

True, you might not always like what you see. Perhaps you realized that you've packed on a few pounds over the winter. But so what? If you see yourself in the world, you'll most likely see other women just like you, too. Maybe we've all packed on a few pounds over the winter. However, they're out there walking, sitting in the cafe or standing in line at the post office, and I bet you'll find a few of these women who are dressed very well and imaginatively. That's the nice thing about struggling with weight—it often forces you to be creative and to appreciate scarves and hats and boots and bijoux.

You see, if we hide out because we're so ashamed, well, that's not going to help you and it's not going to help the community around you, and it just might lead to more comfort eating. So, how about being more like a Frenchwoman? They are rather open and casual about gaining a bit of weight. They don't obsess about dieting. They will actually come right out and tell one another they've gained. But they don't make a big deal about it. They keep in touch with what their body is telling them, whether it's weight gain or loss, and then they make small adjustments over the long term. They just don't go in for the crash diet, because they love and appreciate food too much.

In fact, I recently received an e-mail from Isabelle. When I asked her about body issues, she wrote to me that the most important thing is to feel good in your own skin. The French expression for this is *bien ça peau.* Isabelle suggested that it's important to be able to listen to our bodies, because our bodies will *tell* us what the right weight is for us. No, it's not the numbers on a scale that we should pay most attention to, but it's our very own bodies.

Perhaps it's time to throw out the scale and listen to our thighs, our waist lines, our backs, our bellies, and our derrieres!

City Girls

It seems to me the gals in cities such as New York and Paris are all fairly slim and that's because they have to walk to get anywhere. Even the fat people are slim! You just don't see really overweight people in these cities, because if they carry too much extra weight, it's impossible to get around—to run up and down the subway or Métro steps, to walk the miles that are necessary just to get from point A to point B.

The car can turn into a way of "hiding." It's a little cave, and if you're not careful, it can become a place where you eat those secret candy bars because no one is looking. I think this is why Weight Watchers members will often become leaders once they've reached their goal and want to maintain it over a lifetime. My Cape Cod Weight Watchers leader, the fabulous Barbara, said it was a way for her to keep herself honest. She needed something that would truly keep her invested in her weight control. In a way, she's created a French grandmother for herself out of her Weight Watchers coworkers and members. We are all in this together and we watch out for one another. We're never critical, always accepting, but we also know that it's important to discuss the issues and not be afraid of our excess weight as if it was a terrible monster hiding in the room. This is not only helpful to someone who's struggling, but it demystifies the process of losing and maintaining weight.

It's true, the French are much more likely to tell you if you've gained weight. Here in America, we're much more tactful, but I wonder if in all our tactfulness, we make it a bigger problem. We are so kind and careful and yet, doesn't this skirting of the issue actually compound it by insinuating that weight gain is such an upsetting issue and so private that we are not allowed to ever mention it? I suspect that the success of *Bridget Jones's Diary*—both the book and the movie—can be attributed to the fact that it brought to light this heavy subject in a fun and Everywoman kind of way.

Fat Is the New Thin

Can we put a moratorium on these "miraculous" stories of transformation? You know: "She went from a size fourteen to a size four in twenty-one days!" or "How to lose all that belly fat with one easy trick!"

Recently, I went to a conference and there were mostly women in the audience. The conference had nothing to do with weight loss, but one gal stood up at some point to tell us how she had lost one hundred pounds and was now a size two. Everyone applauded. Honestly, I saw some tears in women's eyes. I was happy for this woman's success, but here's my question. Would she have made this announcement and would we have applauded her if she had lost fifteen pounds? No, I don't think so. And this is because there's no drama in losing fifteen pounds. But I can tell you from personal experience, it's just as hard to lose fifteen pounds as it is to lose fifty pounds. That last fifteen pounds is where the real drama lies. But because we can't "see" it, we don't recognize it. And then there's the appeal of the Cinderella story. Rather than our heroine starting off in rags with a couple of mean stepsisters, she begins her journey as a fat girl. If we're talking about a reality transformation show, she might also need to get her teeth fixed, a new hairdo, all new clothes, liposuction, and breast implants. And then, *voilà!*

She arrives at the ball, transformed. She is beautiful!

Here's the problem with these stories. We are encouraging that black-and-white and either / or mentality. We're sending out the message that daily upkeep—exercise, right food choices, little indulgences, and then little corrections—are just too boring! Why not just wait until we've completely gone to seed, and then have one big operation! Or find a miracle diet. Or hire a fitness guru.

This mentality of being "on the program" or "off the program" will only lead to unhappiness and dissatisfaction and the feeling that we are never good enough. Never perfect. This is not very French and it certainly isn't healthy for the body, mind, or spirit. And if you've lost a lot of weight and then gained it all back and are struggling to lose it once again, well, that can wreak havoc on one's self-esteem. So how about this? How about little steps every day? How about accepting and loving your beautiful, imperfect, fragile self right now, no matter where you are?

This is why I adore the Dove campaign for real beauty. Their message is quite simple—beauty comes in all different shapes, sizes, colors, and ages. If you go to their website, you'll find that Dove is completely dedicated to featuring real women—not airbrushed—in their advertisements. And they've even created a fund supporting girls in their quest to develop self-esteem.

So you see, there's a movement afoot. The truth is companies want to do the right thing and if we let them know that we're unhappy with these unrealistic expectations that constantly confront us in the media, our health and beauty and, yes, even fashion companies will respond. So, speak up. Let the world know that you want to see a wider range of beauty standards. The world is ready to listen!

French Lessons

Decide here and now that you are good enough to eat. There is no such thing as "bad" food and you are not bad for eating food. Do consider portions and how you might eat less and enjoy your food more. Consider staying away from the kitchen between meals and thinking of it as a place that's off limits.

Walk everywhere—it's not only great exercise, but it's a way of being seen in the world and accepting your body right now, not at some future time. Don't fall for those "get thin quick" schemes. Staying slim and healthy is a daily practice. It's not something we turn on or off. And finally, consider becoming a Weight Watcher. There's nothing quite like having an understanding friend to share the experience with you.

Take care of your body for what it is right now, and not at some future date when you reach the dream of perfection. Your body deserves your love in all its permutations. Take the first step toward accepting your body by dressing it up and taking it out for a walk!

CHAPTER EIGHT

Weight Watchers in France

Il y a du pain sur la planche.

(The bread is on the board—meaning we have our work cut out for us.)

FIRST OF ALL, let's get one thing straight: Not all Frenchwomen are skinny.

And maybe it's true that most Parisian women don't get fat, but when you live in France, you will meet plenty of curvy women. In fact, you see women of all shapes and sizes. Although I must admit I did not see truly obese women while in France, but certainly not everyone is oh-so-slim!

However, here's the big difference between the curvy women in France and our American sisters. Frenchwomen—no matter what their size—never give up on beauty and they just don't *act* like they're fat. Beauty is the feminine right of every Frenchwoman, so they would never give it up. In fact, I sense they believe they see it as a duty to their country. After all, they do have a reputation to uphold. And if they need to shed a bit of weight, they might say, *"Oh, I love food*—maybe a little too much, but *c'est la vie!*" They will follow this with the famous French shrug and they will quietly get to work to watch their food, limiting some of their favorite fattening foods, but they will never go completely without. They will simply enjoy a little less cheese, a little less wine, a little less foie gras, *un peu moins de chocolat* (a little less chocolate). But they will never go completely without their little indulgences, because they see the weight issue as a matter of keeping up their figure. Maintenance. It's not an either/or proposition, but rather it involves the daily practice of consciously choosing to be healthy and beautiful. It's this sense of balance that gives them their confidence and their *joie de vivre.* A Frenchwoman will not unhappily sit at a dinner party, feeling miserable, because she can only eat the salad *sans* dressing. She will have a little bit of everything and perhaps make adjustments the next day.

And, honestly, no matter what their size may be, Frenchwomen dress stylishly. They know that if they want to feel good, they need to start by looking good. And so you'll see voluptuous Frenchwomen—especially in the countryside—wearing gorgeous clothes that accent their best features, perhaps an unusually textured knit coat or a beautiful scarf to call attention to their face or eyes, or great bijoux or some one-of-a-kind accessories, such as a hand-knitted cap that they bought directly from an artist at an outdoor market. Oh—and always great shoes or boots!

Of course, many American women do this, too, but I've seen (and I've been actually guilty of this myself) a kind of "giving up" on beauty when we are not exactly where we what to be and we feel we are just too big or too old, so what's the point?

This is how this feeling of defeat can sneak up on us: You're at the hair salon, getting your hair cut and colored. You feel pretty good about that. You think, I'll go shopping after this and buy myself something nice. Perhaps my husband and I will go out to dinner later. As you're waiting for your hair color to set, you pick up the latest copy of *Vogue* and you skim through the pages and look at all the pretty pictures of the impossibly slim and unbelievably young girls, and you brace yourself and say you're okay with that.

However, slowly but surely, you begin to feel a little strange. You begin to feel very, very large and you begin to feel as if these girls in the magazines are from an alien planet. Yes, they belong to the planet of gazellelike bodies, impossibly youthful faces, long thin arms and legs that go on forever and ever. Faces that have never experienced sun damage and hair that is long and silky and smooth and has obviously never experienced a split end. And suddenly, you almost feel like a voyeur, an enormous animal preying on these beauties, stealing them with your glance, and now sitting in the salon, you find yourself transformed into a wooly mammoth creature who, if you were ever to actually encounter one of these cigarette-smoking, Diet Coke–drinking, seven-foot-tall alien girls, you would probably frighten her so much she'd faint from lack of food! And the Fat Police would come and arrest you!

(All right, perhaps that's just my own fear!)

When I am feeling stronger, I realize this: I deserve happiness just as much as anyone else. I realize that perfection is an idea, something that no one will ever attain, and to seek it out is the height of hubris, because after all, we are only human beings and not God. And since I am now *une femme d'un certain âge*, and have acquired just a little bit of wisdom and a lot of patience with myself—I still create goals—I have learned to be much more forgiving when I do not completely reach those goals.

The point is that there is room at this party called life for all of us—whether you are at your goal or near your goal or far from your goal or you really have thrown the idea of goals completely out the window.

Weight Watchers, American Style

I've been going to Weight Watchers on and off since I was fourteen. This means that I've been on and off the program for over forty years, attending meetings in various locations in Connecticut, New York, California, and Massachusetts. In 1985, I became a lifetime member. At the time, I was attending a class in New York City's Upper East Side and after about eight months of following the meal plan, I lost thirty pounds and received a giant gold key and a little plastic card with my lifetime membership number printed on it. This meant I could attend any Weight Watchers meeting, anywhere in the world for free—as long as I never gained more than two pounds over my goal weight, which at the time was 123 pounds.

I now attend meetings on Cape Cod and yes, I have to pay for my meetings (I am definitely two pounds over my goal weight)—although as a lifetime member I do get a little discount, but I would still go whether I got a discount or not. I've been on many programs, but Weight Watchers is the only one that makes sense to me. It's the only one that works for me. And not only that, it's very French! You can eat anything you want. *Really!* You just have to learn about balance. And portion control. Oh, and Weight Watchers are big advocates of walking. *C'est bien français!!*

Serious Business

We are a friendly bunch—my Cape Cod Mashpee Commons Weight Watchers compatriots—but truthfully, sometimes the atmosphere can be a bit somber. Sometimes I feel as if I have sinned and I am there for confession. This is just me, of course, and my imagination. Weight Watchers has no religious affiliations, but I'm a lapsed Catholic (I lapsed at age sixteen, but that's another story). Still, thoughts of sinning and confessions pop up in my brain from time to time. I get this feeling of needing redemption particularly after a holiday, such as Halloween or Thanksgiving or the Fourth of July. I have strayed from the path. I have eaten too much. In fact, I have eaten some *devilishly* good things.

On Wednesday mornings, we "confess." Nobody actually asks us to confess, I just find myself doing it, and I'm not the only one! Some of us at Weight Watchers have forgotten to weigh and measure what we ate. And others have neglected to write down their food intake in the little journals we are provided. We have neglected to exercise, to "work out." We have been lazy and bad and now we are here at Bobby Burns (ironically enough, an Irish pub where our meetings are held) to get weighed and to talk and support one another. Yes, yes, I'm imagining all this confessional business, but there are moments when I cannot help but listen to our Weight Watchers lecturer tell us about the Weight Watchers guidelines and be reminded of the Ten Commandments:

- Drink eight 8-ounce glasses of water every day
- Weigh and measure your food (or at least be aware of portion control)
- Exercise!
- Eat five servings of fruits and vegetables daily
- Eat at least two teaspoons of "healthy" oil each day
- Have two milk products daily (ice cream doesn't count)
- Eat at least one serving of whole grains daily
- Have two lean proteins daily (ice cream is not considered a lean protein)
- Take a multivitamin and a mineral supplement daily
- Limit alcohol and sweets (especially ice cream!)

Okay, they're actually not called "commandments" and no one will accuse you of "sinning" at Weight Watchers, but you get the idea.

The Oil Problem

A lot of the time, we talk about low-point substitutes, low-fat mayonnaise, spray-on "I Can't Believe It's Not Butter," nonfat salad dressing. And with all these nonfat and low-fat substitutes, many women say they can't find a way to fit in the required two teaspoons of oil in their daily diet. The question "How do I fit in the required two teaspoons of oil?" comes up practically every week. I am often tempted to say, just make a salad dressing with some nice extra virgin olive oil and balsamic vinegar, some salt and pepper, and *voilà!* But it would seem that in these ladies' efforts to control calories, they only use premade, store-bought (and not inexpensive) salad dressings with no oil!

And do they taste good?

Well, yes, actually they do, because they may not have any oil in them and they may be nonfat, but they have sugar in them!

Now, I don't think there's anything wrong with a little sugar, but when I have some sugar, I want to know I'm having sugar. I want to enjoy it and feel the *joie de vivre*, so I generally want my sugar in some ice cream or a chocolate fondant or even a little cube in my espresso. The point is, I want to be present for the moment of my sweet indulgence. But you see, the problem with having nonfat salad dressing that's got sugar in it and not even really enjoying the sweetness, is that you think, I haven't had a treat in ages! I haven't had anything sweet! I've been deprived! I deserve a big piece of chocolate cake!

Weight Watchers *à la Française*

I recently attended my Weight Watchers meeting in Toulouse, France. Yes, they have Weight Watchers in France! All over France, women and men are going to Weight Watchers and you know what? They love their Weight Watchers just as much as we do here in America!

But I will tell you this—there's a big difference between Weight Watchers in France and Weight Watchers in America. The program is basically the same, but on French Weight Watchers, they seem to be having more fun than us. Fun talking about food?! Well, yes! And that's because the French love food! They don't have this adversarial relationship to food.

And they don't seem to suffer the same kind of guilt that we often suffer from.

I will never forget the warm October afternoon I walked into the Albert Hotel in Toulouse. I asked where the meeting was being held and a very nice lady told me it was downstairs. Yes, those circular steps again. I found myself in a little meeting room where two ladies were setting up the table and the scales. There was a ragged little line of very talkative women and a few men beginning to form. When I got to the scale, there was some excitement. "Oh, you're from America! We can't weigh you in pounds. Only kilos!" And because of this, they really couldn't tell me whether I had gained or lost weight. As circumstance would have it, a gal from California was in line right behind me and she knew all about translating kilos to pounds. And according to her calculations, I had actually lost a little weight. (This was a bit of a surprise, considering all the baguettes and butter and full-fat yogurt I'd been eating. But then, there was all that walking.)

In fact, later, the leader announced that the topic for the day was *le coeur* (the heart) and she talked about the importance of walking and exercise and how it's good for our heart. She drew a pretty red heart on the flip chart. Ah, love at Weight Watchers! Oh, and she gave all of us—there were about twenty of us—a little pamphlet which had photos showing different ways to exercise: walking, biking, practicing yoga, and dancing. The picture of dancing featured just the legs of a man and a woman doing the tango. The woman in the photos was wearing black high heel pumps and fishnet stockings. You couldn't see her face. The picture focused on the swirling hem of her red silk dress. So even with dieting, there is dance! There is *joie de vivre*! And dare I say, there is the promise of a sexy night out with a mysterious man.

Vive les Américains

My French Weight Watchers leader introduced the lady from California and me to the whole class and told the group that we were a wonderful example of what it means to be true Weight Watchers. After all, here we were, attending our meetings during vacation. I tried to explain that I wasn't exactly on vacation, that I was in France to write, but suddenly we were onto a discussion of how to make a really fine vegetable soup. Recipes were being discussed and exchanged. Everyone talked at once and got very excited. Then we came to "celebrations." This little French Weight Watchers group was doing very well, indeed, losing weight and maintaining. I noticed that there was no applause for individual weight-loss numbers. This was interesting to me because at my American Weight Watchers meeting, we applaud all the time. Really. If you tell them you went on vacation and returned having stayed the same, you get big applause. If you lose an eighth of a pound, you get applause. I actually love all the applause, but I wonder if the Frenchwomen might be better off by not making such a fuss of gains and losses and what's happening with the numbers. It seems they care more about their relationship to eating delicious and healthy food than to what's going on with the scale.

As I could see it, they were a very joyful and optimistic group. The only difficulty seemed to be occasionally making the choice of one food and foregoing another. At one point, a lady in the back revealed that she had had a difficult week. She was feeling *un peu découragée* (a little discouraged). She had been to a dinner party and everything was so delicious and tempting! She then proceeded to talk about all the food, but it was difficult to understand what she was saying because the ladies and the one man erupted into laughter and discussion, talking over one another and really getting excited. Finally, the leader waved her hands and made this pronouncement: *Vous pouvez prendre le saucisson ou le foie gras, mais vous ne pouvez pas prendre les deux.* ("You can have the *saucisson* or the foie gras, but you can't have both.") How wise! How simple! Truthfully, this was so funny and so fabulous to me. Because if it were me, I wouldn't have either the foie gras or the *saucisson.* I'd have the salad. And then, after a week of doing that, I'd probably break down and have the foie gras *and* the *saucisson*! Nowadays this pronouncement has become a kind of mantra for me. We have to make choices in life. You can have the sausage or the foie gras, but you can't have both. You can have the ice cream or you can have the apple pie, but you can't have both.

This was a bit of a departure from my American Weight Watchers experience. In all the meetings I've attended around the country, I have never heard the members talk so tenderly about real food. Yes, my sister American Weight Watchers will go on and on about this product that has twenty grams of fiber and zero grams of fat and only twenty calories for an entire bagful, but it seems to me they just don't really love their food the way the French love their food.

These French Weight Watchers really found great *joie de vivre* in every piece of cheese, every tomato, every glass of wine. Perhaps in the past, they enjoyed all these things too much and that's why they've found themselves at Weight Watchers. Still, the French meetings seemed to be a celebration of what *can* be eaten. In a certain way, I suspect that the portion control and limitations that come from being on the Weight Watchers plan actually give the French an opportunity to get even more over the moon when it comes to appreciating the delicate charms of a strawberry or the earthy appeal of a mushroom. There was so much excitement in the room, and the women were actually talking very fast and occasionally over one another. I must say this was a fun change from my American Weight Watchers meeting where Barbara, our leader, often struggles to get anyone to talk at all!

Food Talk

Whether you're in a Weight Watchers group or not, consider that talking about food can be the first step to honoring what you put in your body. Food is good. Yes, it is not a demon. It is not your adversary—well, not when it is handled with care and respect and love. If you think about your food and you talk about what you love to eat, then by the time you prepare it and sit down to eat it, you have awakened your senses. As you stand at your stove and stir the pot of fresh vegetables and inhale the aroma of garden tomatoes and green beans, and then take a taste, you might decide, yes, that's enough salt, or perhaps a little more. If you use sea salt or something rare and fine such as *fleur de sel* (hand-harvested sea salt from the coast of Brittany), this gives you a moment to truly appreciate what you are preparing. Yes, sea salt is expensive and so you mustn't take this meal for granted. When you take your time, and add love to the recipe, well, then you simply can't wolf it down. And you can't overeat.

The Language of Food

Remember my American expat friend Marjorie—the radio documentary producer who sings jazz? She's been living in France for the last twenty years. When I knew her in New York City, she was one of those tall, skinny girls (a real Audrey Hepburn look-alike) who could eat anything (cheeseburgers and fries!) and still stay skinny. She had an amazing metabolism that I honestly envied. However, as she's become a bit older, she's found she needs to be more careful. I love her attitude toward food, because she doesn't possess the emotional baggage that comes from having struggled with weight control for her entire life (like me!). Rather, she's very openhearted when it comes to her diet. Oh, and she goes to Weight Watchers in France. She's been doing it for years. Here's what she has to say about her Weight Watchers meeting in Lille:

> I love Weight Watchers in French! You know very well that one of the important principles of WW is to enjoy food, and to take pleasure in its preparation. Well, that is something that is already there in the culture—talking about ordinary bits of food put artfully together and taking a reverent amount of time to partake of them is just normal. The French don't have the problem of throwing down food without tasting that I think a large part of the U.S. does. They give each course its due. So when the

> *animatrice* [the leader] starts talking about some fruit or vegetable she's featuring that week, and the girls start sharing recipes, they can really go to town. And this is where the language comes in—*des petits pois légèrement salés* or *une tranche de brioche tartinée* sound like something very special to me, versus green peas with a little salt, or a slice of bread spread with something. It's just by translating it into French that it seems more desirable, but it isn't because it reminds me of a French restaurant. It's more because for me, as the language enters my brain and takes over, and I leave the shore behind, I suddenly swim in my experiences with friends around a table, the dinner that took four hours, the meal that was the main event in itself.

So we've returned to the dinner party once again. It seems obvious that the dinner party is a place where romance blooms, families bond, friendships are strengthened, and community forms, but now we see that the dinner party is also the secret to the French ability to stay slim (or at least not gain too much weight!).

When a dinner party or even an ordinary family dinner takes hours, you certainly cannot mindlessly binge. First of all, people are watching. Second of all, each course is served one at a time, on little plates. You have no choice but to take your time and really enjoy what's before you. If you have some chicken, that's all that's on your plate. And you may spend twenty minutes eating that little piece of chicken. It's considered impolite to ask for seconds and why would you, when you can be sure that there will be more little plates of delicious food. Perhaps next comes a plate of *haricot verts* (green beans). And again, you will spend twenty minutes eating them. In between, you will talk and laugh and even argue. You will sip some wine. And some water. And then there will be a plate of salad. A cheese course. And so on. Because you are concentrating on one type of food at a time, you learn to truly savor the individual flavors. It seems to me this way of eating is easy to replicate here in the United States. All you need is to use those little plates, slow down, talk in between, drink wine, then water, and eat one food at a time.

Hungry for Love

Here's the problem when we get into an adversarial relationship with food: it leads to that either/or mentality. We are on a diet and we are good. We may not be happy. We may miss eating delicious food, but we're good. We're angels, in fact. The problem with this is if we "slip" and have a little ice cream, or butter, or we really enjoy that apple tart—well, then we are bad. This leads to a kind of self-loathing. For me, I know that I'm often "good" in public. And then after a few weeks of deprivation and feeling as if I can't take it anymore, I am "bad." I binge. And then I hate myself and I hate the food that has led me astray. I've analyzed this pattern over and over again. I've come to the conclusion that I use food for emotional healing, for love. And I've tried to find ways to find this comfort elsewhere. When I feel stress, I've taken bubble baths to relax, gone for a brisk walk to get the endorphins going. I've taken a nap when I feel emotionally drained. I've developed my version of the Secret Garden. Now, I don't think there's anything wrong with this approach, but after traveling to France and becoming close to Frenchwomen, I've come to realize that food really is a form of love and no one is apologetic about this! To prepare food is an act of love. To make a wonderful meal for your friends and family is a form of love. To enjoy someone's delicious meal is a way of loving. And certainly, food plays an essential role in the art of seduction!

In America, we are told that food is not love, and should not be used as such, because this is what has gotten us curvy girls into trouble in the first place. But I would like to make a radical proposal: Let's say that food *is love.* If this is the case, then let's treat our food and our bodies with genuine respect. Let's feed our bodies delicious, artfully prepared, healthy, fresh food. Let's not be promiscuous with our food—eating indiscriminately, indulging in fast food that does not really satisfy. Simply put, let's put love back into the equation and see what happens.

For me, having just returned from France, I know this: Loving food does not lead to overeating; it leads to eating just enough. And it leads to a feeling of well-being. Yes, and happiness.

French Lessons

START BY LOVING your body as it is right now. Feel comfortable in your own skin by luxuriating in fragrance and lotions, taking bubble baths, and dressing well. That's the French way.

Enjoy your food. You have a right to eat, and it's actually helpful to "come out of the closet" and talk about food and recipes and actually love your food. Once you love food, you'll be less likely to "abuse" it. The best way to love your food is to experiment with new recipes and to host dinner parties. When you eat in front of others, you'll be less likely to diet in public and binge in private. Enjoy real food, rather than processed or nonfat or foods with sugar substitutes. You'll be more satisfied and less likely to feel deprived.

Find friends who understand your struggle and with whom you can share your stories and recipes. I highly recommend Weight Watchers. Truly, over the long term, it's the only program that really works. And that's because it's not a diet, it's a way of living and finally making peace with your body and food.

Frenchwomen don't diet. They don't think they're "bad" when they indulge. And you're not "bad," either. So you ate too much food—so what? You will now eat a little less. The truth is, if you allow yourself to truly appreciate your food and speak lovingly about it (the way Frenchwomen do), you will end up eating less, because you will bring a new awareness to each bite.

Take one day at a time and enjoy the process. No one is perfect! Find the *joie de vivre* in where you are right now, in this very moment.

CHAPTER NINE

How to Flirt à la Française

> I don't understand how a woman can leave the house without fixing herself up a little—if only out of politeness. And then, you never know, maybe that's the day she has a date with destiny. And it's best to be as pretty as possible for destiny.
>
> —COCO CHANEL

THE FRENCH DON'T actually have a word for "flirt." This is because every conversation, every encounter, every look, every small negotiation, every apple that is purchased, every baguette that is bought involves what we might consider a teeny bit of "flirting." France is a country layered in tradition and subtext. For example, in the past, shops were located in the street level of a person's house, so when you walked in, you were actually entering their "home." Because of this, it was considered rude to just walk in and start fingering the merchandise without engaging in a little greeting, perhaps a little conversation, and at the very least, a hearty *"Bonjour, madame!"* or *"Bonjour, monsieur!"*

"Flirting" became a way to smooth the road, so to speak,

and has been used in business as well as pleasure. You see, flirting for the French is not exactly what we think of as flirting. It has nothing to do with seduction or teasing (at least not most of the time). It's more about the art of conversation, which is highly valued in the country. This art of conversation is all about being polite, recognizing that you are participating in an age-old social exchange. Plus, it transforms the business of life into something that is a little more fun and yes, more delicious.

Our Frenchwoman will "flirt" with her eyes, looking up, then quickly down, then up again. She will "flirt" by getting into an agreeable disagreement. She will "flirt" by softly laughing. She is flirting simply by the way she walks into a room, the way she brushes her hair to the side, the way she crosses her legs, the way she deprives you of her brilliant smile until she deems you worthy of seeing her perfectly imperfect white teeth. And she "flirts" with everyone all the time. And so because there is no ending or beginning, you cannot feel she is turning it on or turning it off. It is her way of being present to the world. It's what makes her happy. It's part of her *joie de vivre.*

Les Bisous

Last spring, I found myself on the Paris Métro watching a small group of French teenagers chatting. There were five of them—three boys and two girls and they must have been about sixteen years old. I watched as they met up and greeted one another by a kiss on each cheek. This took quite a while—since the train was crowded and we were all standing. Once the kisses were over, they got down to the business of being young people—laughing and flirting and talking about school.

But back to the all-important *les bisous* (kisses). It seemed to me that the world as we know it—the new millennium—stopped for a moment while two of the boys and the two girls participated in an age-old ritual that has been handed down from generation to generation. I couldn't help but think how this small gesture must create a kind of groove in the French brain, a kind of riverbed, where the manners flow. And more than this, it's such an intimate gesture. It's so much more gentle and intimate than the handshake or whatever young people are doing as a way of greeting at this moment in time. I know my daughter and her friends hug one another, but I still think the cheek kiss is sweeter and demands more care and precision. After all, if you are too quick, you will miss the mark, so it forces an individual to focus on the present moment.

Little Children

The Métro stopped and on came a mother and her little daughter. The girl must have been about three years old. She stood there, holding her mother's hand and immediately focused in on the teenagers. Well, one teenager in particular. The boy—actually, the cutest boy. And as the train stopped and let out the two girls, the three-year-old girl smiled at the teenage boy. He smiled back. And then, she hid behind her mother's skirt. The train continued on and she peeked out, once again staring at the boy and then in a flash, I saw her do something incredible. She batted her eyelashes. He laughed. And the train moved on.

What a delightful moment. It was pure innocence. And yet, this little girl and this teenage boy were practicing "the flirt."

Now, of course, little girls all over the world are flirting and laughing and smiling and fascinated by older children.

However, I wonder if, as American girls, we are eventually taught to stop. Are we taught that it's dangerous? Are we told that it will lead to misunderstandings later on in life?

Yet it doesn't seem to be a problem with the French. And so, it's made me think that perhaps there's something to the formality of *les bisous* as a way of framing human interactions. After all, you first learn to kiss your mother, your father, your brother or sister or grandmother. *La bise* blends family love with friendship and flirtation. These kisses are not separated into different categories and I suspect *la bise* may just be the secret to their *ooh la la*, their mystery and sexiness. For a Frenchwoman, love and affection is not an either/or proposition. The kiss is not a quick sloppy thing. It is quite formal. And when you combine this formality with the attention to language—the *vous* for the formal "you" and the *tu* for the familiar "you," as well as being greeted so often as a *mademoiselle* or *madame*—well, I believe this creates a certain tension between the intimate and the familiar. Perhaps even a challenge. The *la bise* greeting means that Frenchwomen and men must be affectionate and physical on a daily basis. Just think what all this gentle kissing-greeting does to their endorphins!

The First Kiss

With all this daily kissing, you might think that the first time a boy and girl kiss is no big deal. Actually, the first time a boy and girl kiss *on the lips* is a very big deal.

During my day of helping to harvest the grapes, the lovely teenager Manon explained to me how she had met her boyfriend, Laurent—the son of the owners of the vineyard and winery. Later, Manon (now seventeen) sent me this e-mail describing how she and Laurent first met.

> First of all, we were together at school, at the *lycée.* I was fifteen and he was seventeen years old.
>
> Something sad had happened the day before, and I was so sad at school. I had only spoken to Laurent twice in my life. We had some friends in common, but I didn't really know him. He was cute and funny, but I knew that other girls were interested in him so I didn't care. The day that I felt really bad, I was outside in the garden of our school, he was also there. We started to talk. He made me laugh, while my friends tried unsuccessfully all day long. The only one who could make me smile was Laurent.
>
> In the evening, I was back at home, and I went on my computer and Laurent spoke to me on MSN [chat] because he had heard that I had been sad, but he couldn't understand because I was laughing with him the whole afternoon, he couldn't believe his ears!
>
> So I told him everything, and he said that if I wanted, he could phone me that night. So we spoke until the morning. Every evening we did the same for a whole month. We got to know each other very well. We were laughing all the time together.
>
> My friends said that I was falling in love but I didn't believe it.
>
> After nearly two months of conversations, we knew that we were really attracted to each other. Then he told me that when he saw me during the first day of

> school he decided I was the most beautiful girl he had ever seen . . . on Thursday the 6th of May in 2008, we went for a walk far from the school to be alone, without all those children looking at us and wondering what was going on. We were at a football stadium, not really romantic, but enough for us. We were talking, laughing, he held my hand while we were talking. I was chewing on some gum that tasted like blackcurrant. Laurent says he will always remember this smell. I also had some lemon-flavored lipgloss on my lips. We will never forget this. While we were talking, we were quite close to each other, I couldn't wait, I kissed him, he smiled, he gave me a hug and that's how it started.
>
> I met Laurent's parents two months after starting this love relationship. Now, two years later, we're still together, it's still fine, we're still in love, and next year we'll live together in a little apartment because I go to the university and he is there already. We are young, but we hope that it will continue as it is now.

I loved Manon's story. First of all, it describes that magic of first love, true love. Manon is an extraordinarily beautiful young lady, but more than this, she is modest and self-possessed and even a little mysterious.

The first real kiss between a boy and a girl is an important step toward a romance. *La bise*—the kiss on each cheek in greeting, adds to the tension between formality and intimacy.

A Kiss Is Still a Kiss

But it's just a kiss! A way of greeting. And here it is—completely available to you, as an American woman. In fact, many of us already greet with the kiss on each cheek. For many years, I greeted friends and family this way. I know that some people found it curious and maybe even a little old-fashioned, but it felt so natural to me. Now I realize, it's just something my grandmother and mother did and so I did it, too. And it's really a lovely greeting. It's more feminine than the handshake and not as physically direct as the hug. Start by giving your close friends and family the kiss on the cheek. Take your time and do it with a sense of purposefulness. Observe how it makes you feel. Be in the moment. This is not a Hollywood air kiss. This is a sincere moment of greeting.

If it feels awkward to kiss *à la française*, then start by just giving them a little peck on the right cheek. This may sound silly or trivial, but this tiny gesture has the capacity to change your life. Imagine the atoms that are floating through the air. When you are cheek to cheek, you feel the person's breath close to you, and for a moment you even hear the sound of the heart beating. And if you are kissing someone who is secretly attracted to you and you to them, this kiss on the cheek will gently part the curtains to slowly reveal something more.

Make an Entrance

Flirting is really just an attitude. It begins with the way you feel about yourself and your place in the world. We've all known a woman who is not particularly beautiful; she doesn't have a perfect figure, she's not amazingly talented or intelligent, and yet all the men she meets fall a little bit in love with her. She doesn't dress provocatively, really, but everyone agrees, she's very, very sexy. What's her secret? It's simple: She *believes* she is sexy. She *believes* she is beautiful.

Frenchwomen often possess this kind of confidence. This sense of self starts in childhood when they are taught proper posture through dance lessons. They will take plenty of time with the rituals of the bath and love smoothing their skin with fragrant lotion, and then spritzing on their signature perfume. A Frenchwoman will wear beautiful lingerie—every day. She wears it for herself and for her pleasure, not necessarily to impress a man. Oh, and she'll often wear high heels.

Before a woman even enters a room, she announces her approach through the sound of her heels. Yes, *before* she even arrives. It's similar to that feeling of expectation we get when we are sitting in a theater, waiting for the play to begin and the orchestra begins to play the overture. *Click-click, clock, click, click, click, clock, click.* This is particularly apparent when the woman approaching is walking on cobblestone streets or a tile floor. This sound is more than a little hypnotic. It builds anticipation. And then there is the subtle hint of fragrance. Something associated only with this woman. Something rare and fine and intoxicating. You see, already, she has begun to cast her spell on us.

A Frenchwoman will not rush into the room with her head bowed, full of apologies and saying, "I'm sorry!" for being late. No. Rather, she will stand at the door and "frame" herself. She will wait until you see her. She will not make her approach until she is noticed. And then, she will make her grand entrance, knowing she is being watched. She will smile, and walk slowly, head up, shoulders back, stomach in, just as her *mère* (mother) taught her. She will take her time to greet everyone and make eye contact. This is where *les bisous* add to the enchantment. And if she is wearing a scarf, she will take her time unwrapping it in such a way that has you completely mesmerized.

Oh, and she doesn't apologize for being ten minutes late and actually it doesn't matter, because by this time, everyone has forgotten about this and besides, her entrance was worth the wait.

At a dinner party in Auvillar, John Alexander, a photographer and writer from Vancouver who spends as much time as possible in France, describes the magic of heels this way:

> From the fifth-floor window in the narrow street canyons of Paris, late at night, the unmistakable sound of a woman's high heels on the cobblestones is evocative. Louder as she approaches, diminishing as she moves away, it's as though all of *Casablanca* is played out in those ten or twenty seconds.

Is the simple act of walking and entering a room a form of flirtation? Yes, absolutely. It's about how you present yourself. And this way of flirting is available to all of us. No matter how shy you are, you can begin to learn the art of enchantment by simply taking your time to walk into a room.

Practice this when there is nothing at stake. For instance, you're walking into your local cafe or coffee shop. Slowly open the door, with your head held high, your shoulders back. Then, pause a moment and look around the room. Take in the visual feast. Then, breathe deeply and walk slowly to a table or the counter. Smile slightly. All this may sound too simple, too easy, but if you repeat this little exercise often, you will start to build the kind of confidence that Frenchwomen possess. You will find yourself feeling generally more calm and self-possessed.

And then, when it comes to an occasion where you want to make a grand entrance, you will know exactly how to do it.

Art Class

It's true Frenchwomen have a bit of an advantage on us. Every day, in the parks and on the streets, in the big cities and the little villages, they are surrounded by reminders of how beautiful the world finds the female form. There are sculptures of glorious classic nudes that announce to anyone with eyes that women are beautiful. We are loved. We are as important and as necessary to life as the air we breathe. And Woman is appreciated for a myriad of forms—yes, there are sculptures of slender ballerinas, but more than this, you will see lusciously voluptuous females and monuments to muscled heroines.

You may not live in Paris and perhaps there are no statues or public art in your town to build up your sense of confidence and beauty, but you can still borrow a bit of confidence and self-love by a visit to your local art gallery or art museum. Take your time and really *look* at the paintings of the impressionists, the classic statues. See yourself through a man's eye. Do this on a regular basis. Not only will you build your confidence, but also you'll learn something new about art and life.

Have Fun

So, you see, flirting is about so much more than witty repartee, amusing bon mots, and clever comebacks. As Americans we're often told it's not nice to "flirt" and that flirting is a form of teasing. But this way of flirting is not about teasing anyone, but about being strong and confident and self-assured. In France it's considered polite to flirt, to be charming, and it's considered a compliment to the person of the opposite sex. It's also a necessary part of French life. Certainly, the French dinner party is fueled by lively, fun, and flirty conversation.

How do you learn to flirt? Start by practicing in your own town. Talk to shop owners. Ask questions. Get into conversations on topics you're passionate about. Learn how to play with language. Anybody can flirt and sometimes you'll find it's very helpful to neutralize a potentially tricky situation. In fact, not too long ago I was in New York City, dogsitting an adorable little Maltese named Charlie. My instructions were to take Charlie to the local deli on Eighty-fourth and Amsterdam every evening where he would be given a scrap of meat from Bob the proprietor. Now, one evening I went in and I realized there was actually a sign on the door that said NO DOGS. But my friend has told me that this was something they were used to and this sign did not apply to Charlie. Well, I felt very nervous this night, worried they were going to kick us out of the store. And to top it off, while I was waiting in line at the counter, Charlie began barking. A man turned around and looked at me. (Charlie was hidden under the counter.) Clearly I had been caught. So, I looked at the man and said, "There's no dog here. I'm a ventriloquist!" Well, that defused the situation and the man laughed and Charlie got his treat. And then I realized that the man was waiting at the door. When he realized I wasn't going to say anything further to him, he just said, "Well, good-bye, gals!" And left. I thought of telling him that Charlie is a guy not a gal, but then I didn't want to get into any more of this flirtation. I am a married woman, after all!

But here's the point—I left that store feeling somehow happier. That little encounter gave me a whole lot of *joie de vivre.* But I didn't walk into the store thinking, I'm going to flirt with a stranger tonight. Rather, I was just going about my business and enjoying my life and even being in this little predicament and having to come up with something to get me out of a slightly sticky situation.

Flirting with the Cheese Man

Many Frenchwomen said that their secret to flirtation was just to be friendly and to have fun. I saw a great example of this at the market in Valence d'Agen. I was there with my friend, the American writer Denise Emanuel Clemen. She wanted to buy some cheese to bring back to the artists colony and so she approached the cheese man. What a funny, gregarious fellow! We had actually met him earlier in the morning at the outdoor cafe where he was having an espresso, so the flirtation had already begun. By the time we stood before his selection of cheeses, it felt as if we were old friends. In fact, the cheese man insisted on giving Denise little samples of a variety of delicious cheeses. He described each one in poetic detail and, of course, Denise bought quite a bit of cheese that day. (So he was not only a good flirt, but also a smart businessman.) But what was surprising was how he asked about her marital status by simply taking her hand, noting that there was no ring there, and then asking her how it was possible that she was not taken. She explained that yes, in fact she was single. Newly divorced. And you know, he asked her to go out with him that evening. Clearly, he was smitten by the charming and beautiful Denise.

In the end, she declined, but this little encounter brought such a sense of joy to her entire day and, in fact, that evening at the dinner party, we told everyone about the very amorous and adorable cheese man. So you can see, flirting can be very indirect. When you're talking about cheese or the weather or if you think that new book is any good, you can be flirting. It's a matter of being friendly and having fun. Nothing is more appealing than a woman who looks like she's having a good time and enjoying life. And as you can see with Denise's experience, flirting is a way to connect to your community, your town or village, and your home.

Get Physical

Flirting can be the simple act of listening. If you are a really good listener, you are a natural charmer. And if you feel you are not a good listener, practice it. Begin by simply leaning forward a bit. Smile. You might gently touch the man's hand or even brush against his sleeve. Frenchwomen tend to hold back on their smiles, but if you're an American, it's kind of expected. Oh, and the French find our smiles *trés charmant*. (very charming). We're known to be an open and effusive culture, so why not enjoy it and give the world your dazzling smile. Go ahead and laugh. You don't have to hold back.

And if you want to take this one step further, you can show a particular man that you're approachable by sending out subtle signals, such as playing with your necklace or gently brushing your bangs away from your face. You might use a little body language and show the open palm of your hand. You might wear an open neckline. Certainly, a well-timed smile and a meaningful look in the eye is a form of flirting. However, all of these techniques only work if you are careful not to "turn it on and then turn it off." It's important to strive to develop your own style and to be consistent.

Words of Wisdom from an Expert Flirter

Lisa Solod is the editor of a wonderful and very moving book, *Desire: Women Write About Wanting*. She's also a widely published essayist and short story writer. Lisa writes online for blogcritics.com and the Huffington Post. And more than this, Lisa is a great supporter of women writers (me, included!) and she's a total Francophile, having lived in Paris for a number of years. Oh, and she's a natural flirt—in the most subtle and delightful way. When you meet the charming Lisa, you can't even tell she's flirting with you, but you leave the encounter feeling happy to be alive and in this world. And so, she's the perfect person to ask about flirting. Here's what she had to say:

> On the eve of our separation, my ex-husband complained (admitted?) that the only reason anyone came to our wildly popular dinner parties was down to me. He attributed it to my "personality" which, on good occasions, he admired. I would be quicker to

explain the attraction by owning, which I finally do (wholeheartedly), my flirtatious nature.

I flirt with everyone: men, women, children, even tiny babies (if I can't get a screaming baby to smile, then something is deeply wrong). It's second nature to me, flirting, and I neither turn it on nor off. I certainly expect nothing from it other than whatever response I would wish from someone I was merely talking to. Because for me, flirting *is* talking. As a matter of fact, it might be more like, well, breathing. It is simply my way of negotiating the world I live in and an intrinsic part of who I am. Had no one pointed it out specifically I might not even have been able to put a name to it.

Bill Clinton, whatever one thinks of him, is a master flirt. Even people who were not fans describe talking with him as a singular experience: he looks his companion right in the eye and makes him or her feel as though he or she is the only person in the room. That's how flirting works: the eye/face/person attention is so pure that the person with whom one is flirting can't help but feel special, if only for a moment.

People give flirting a bad name, and perhaps if one is deliberately obvious about it for personal gain, then it isn't a good thing. On the other hand, that sort of flirting isn't really flirting, in any pure sense. When I flirt, I am intent on making that one-on-one connection. It is the only thing on which I am concentrating: flirting is something I do whenever I

> meet someone who interests me, for whatever reason. Like my brown eyes and big breasts, I think it's a genetic trait. If people can be genetically shy, why can't they be genetically flirtatious? I wouldn't have it any other way.

And neither should you!

Talk About Love

One of the first things I learned during my French tutorials with Marceline is that the French do not pronounce their consonants the way we do in English. Everything feels softer to me. Even a simple word like *petit.* If you were to say this in English, you would stop and pronounce that last T, letting your tongue hit the roof of your mouth. But in French, you actually completely drop the last T. It seems to me that consonants are frequently dropped off, as if the French speaker got distracted and drifted into another thought. Or perhaps that's my imagination. Still, I do think this contributes to the delicious swooshing and *shhh-shhh-shhh* sound of the language. There's so much mystery to the language. Often, I'll hear a word spoken and then when I see it written, I'm surprised to find that it ends with a T or an N.

Now, if you speak English, you might feel your language is precise and your consonants are strong. If you want to borrow a little "Frenchness," the answer isn't to start slurring your words or droppings your Ns and Ts. But how about this: Pay attention to your words. Modulate your voice. Strive to speak musically. We have a beautiful language that is influenced by Latin origins (as the French language is), as well as the German language. Some of our words have harder sounds and some have softer sounds, so it's important to appreciate your language and the nuances of words. And, lucky us, we actually have many more words to chose from than the French! So why not use them carefully and enjoy the power of your own language. Protect your language and don't take it for granted.

By understanding the full power of your own language, with all its complexities, you will create an unbeatable and sexy combination. You'll have that American can-do spirit, that openness, that friendliness, plus the sexy-soft-sweetness that is so inviting when you know a little more about the power of your own language.

French Lessons

Become involved in your community. Begin by walking everywhere and visiting your favorite shops on a regular basis. Build up your confidence by always greeting the shop owners with an enthusiastic "hello!"

Don't worry about "flirting," but rather develop your conversational skills by asking questions. This is where practicing on shop owners is great—they welcome your questions about their wares. Another way to practice the art of conversation is to simply compliment both men and women. Look for easy ways to compliment someone. Say something nice about their shoes or briefcase, their umbrella or hat. When you know them better, you can tell them about their fabulous smile or sexy eyes.

If you feel it's appropriate, you might gently touch someone's hand or arm or sleeve. You don't have to be French to greet a friend or acquaintance with a light kiss on the cheek.

Think romantic thoughts. I know this might sound crazy, but I've practiced it and it really works. I do this around my husband and the next thing you know, he's touching me and kissing me and this begins a night of romance and I didn't have to say a thing!

Wear good lingerie all the time. For yourself. It's a terrific confidence booster.

Be conscious of your own body when you enter a room. Think about the musicality of your heels clicking on the floor, your speaking voice, and the language you use and your whisper. Appreciate the power of a look, the flutter of eyelashes, and your smile.

Finally, develop your posture—if you can, take dance lessons. Practice your entrance into a room. Go to an art gallery and let all the voluptuaries in art fill you with confidence and *joie de vivre.*

CHAPTER TEN

I See London, I See France

Dreams are necessary to life.
—ANAÏS NIN

BACK IN THE LATE 1960S, graduating from elementary school and going on to the seventh grade was a big moment in every young woman's life. It meant you were now in the school with the big kids, but it also meant you could ditch the babyish white ankle socks and wear nylon stockings. I will never forgot the Sunday night before I was to begin my first day at junior high school.

My grandmother came to visit on Sunday, as always, but I didn't have the heart to tell her I didn't want my hair done in ringlets—it was so out of fashion by this point—and so I let her make rag curls for me. And as my hair was drying in my bedroom, she whispered that she had a gift for me for the first day of school, now that I was no longer a baby, but becoming a young lady. She took out a small paper shopping bag from Howland's. I opened the bag, thinking, she is giving me a new dress or sweater—poor boy tops were in fashion and hip-hugger skirts with wide belts. Beatle boots and white lipstick and Love's Fresh Lemon cologne.

But no, it was none of these things. It was a pale pink girdle. It wasn't even a new girdle. In fact, it was her old girdle. True, she had washed it and it was as fresh as can be, but she was thrifty so it was not new. I sat there on my bed and held the thing up before me and thought, Oh my God, the thing is so small. How the heck will I fit into it? It looked like something made for my Patty Playpal doll. And then my grandmother explained to me how it stretches and she demonstrated, reassuringly pulling out the sides. "It'll keep that tummy in," she said, adding, "ladies never go out without a girdle. And it's good for your posture!"

I was actually more than a little thrilled by this gift. The thought that this little girdle would "hold me in" made me happy. And I imagined I would not be like my mother, who was becoming a little crazy and definitely out of control. Now that I was starting seventh grade, I would be like my elegant grandmother and I would be studying French!

I wore the girdle to the first day of school along with my new nylon stockings.

I will say this—I don't remember anything of the first day of seventh grade except for being in excruciating pain. I had such a stomachache, I could think of nothing else but getting the damn girdle off of me. On my way home from school, I rolled it down around my hips and walked—or should I say waddled—home with my friends Joanne and Cornelia and they laughed at me. They thought it was hysterical. Why was I wearing a girdle!? Who did I think I was?! Was I crazy? But they didn't understand and I couldn't tell them. I wore the girdle because I was striving for something beyond Stamford, Connecticut, beyond Dolan Junior High School, beyond Connecticut or even New York City. This girdle was my entry into something foreign and *French.*

By the time I got to the eighth grade, nylon stockings were replaced with pantyhose, which we wore with our hip huggers and miniskirts. And by the time I graduated from high school in 1971 we were wearing jeans and going braless. Silk slips, delicate garter belts, pink girdles, and sheer nylon stockings were fripperies of the past. Or at least something only your French grandmother might wear, understanding that the nature of *joie de vivre* when it comes to lingerie is not always about what makes you feel comfortable, but more about what makes you feel confident.

The Red Slip Society

There's a legend that when Flo Ziegfeld began producing the famed Ziegfeld Follies, he gave each of his showgirls seventy-five dollars (a small fortune in the 1920s) to go out and buy some beautiful lingerie. This lingerie was not meant to be worn for the big extravaganza of feathers and sequins and spectacular evening gowns, but rather to wear every day—to make the woman feel beautiful and elegant on a daily basis. He understood that for a woman, sexuality couldn't be something that is easily turned on or off. Rather, there should be a slow-burning flame of desirability all the time. So, in a way, this purchase of good lingerie was an important investment in his showgirls' sense of beauty and confidence. And this confidence was something they could take from their ordinary lives and bring it with them into the limelight.

For me, this secret confidence booster is a simple red slip.

I wear a lot of black and it was a French girl who told me about the power of wearing my red slip under a black dress. Nowadays, particularly when I speak, I am sure to wear the red slip. And there's been a great deal of reaction to the red slip. In fact, I received a lovely note from a lingerie shop in California called Farr West. They have a number of very sexy red silk chemise slips. Yes, slips are old-fashioned and out of style. Yes, my daughter and her friends will actually wear vintage slips as evening dresses, but for me, I still remember when a slip was a slip. It was something you wore to keep a dress from being completely sheer in the sunlight. Today this seems quaint, but there was a time when ladies wouldn't go out without a slip. Same as with the girdle.

I cannot help but think that there is something lost in all this throwing off of intimate garments. Yes, we are more relaxed, we are free from encumbrances and layers and ties and buckles and bindings, but has this truly added to our confidence? Or do we sometimes feel just a little bit naked? A little undressed? And certainly between the girdle and before the advent of Spanx, we were left feeling a little vulnerable in our fleshiness. Perhaps this is why toning and fitness and Pilates classes have become so popular. Nothing wrong with that, but sometimes I even miss that little pink girdle that my grandmother gave me, or at least the idea of it.

I wonder if there is some part of our national psyche that misses the complications of wearing lingerie and feminine foundations on a daily basis. Why else would the women of *Mad Men* create such a stir? Just look at Christina Hendricks playing the oh-so-voluptuous Joan Holloway. Men go absolutely crazy for this Amazonian beauty and I'm sure it's in large part due to the form-fitting dresses and the body underneath that is clearly held in and up with all the intimate accoutrements available to a woman during the late fifties and early sixties.

What Transvestites Can Tell Us

As Americans, we do have a tendency to go overboard, to lose our balance and we're no different when it comes to our underwear. But a certain population has never forgotten the charms of beautiful underthings. Yes, while we were flamboyantly discarding girdles and stockings, gay men and transvestites were quietly collecting them. I recently interviewed Sandi Simon from Bra Smyth in New York City. Her daughters Becky Simon and Diana Simon now own the stores, but she told me how back in the early seventies when she took over her father's lingerie shop in the Bronx (then called Frishman's Corset and Lingerie) her clientele included the waves of new immigrants coming to the United States, as well as cross-dressers in search of the vintage underthings their mothers wore. And during the era when breast cancer was spoken of only in hushed tones and there was a certain kind of shame and secrecy, Frishman's was one of the few lingerie shops that fit women for mastectomy bras and swimsuits, along with prosthetics, since implants were still not commonplace.

Today, Sandi helps her daughters at their two Bra Smyth locations—one on the East Side of Manhattan and one on the West Side. These two amazing shops bridge the gap between sensible foundation wear and frilly lingerie. They have all kinds of Spanx accessories, as well as a service to fit bras to the individual woman. In fact, Bra Smyth has an actual tailor on the premises that will custom fit a bra for you! How very French! Yes, French, because for the French, fashion is all about classic design and the absolutely perfect fit. They have fine French lingerie from all the major French designers, including Simone Perele, Chantelle, Barbara, Lise Charmel, and Aubade.

Lingerie in Your Own Backyard

And you don't have to travel to France or even New York City to find good French lingerie. In fact, I recently found two great little shops right here on the Cape. We have Katherine Hudson's own shop, K M Hudson, in Mashpee and Ladybird Lingerie on Nantucket. Melissa, the manager, tells me that they are one of the few distributors in the United States for the French brand Princesse Tam Tam (a big favorite among the Frenchwomen I interviewed!). French Dressing in Boston's Beacon Hill neighborhood and Bedroom I's Boutique in Osterville, Massachusetts, also have a great selection of fine French lingerie. The owner of Bedroom I's, Aimee Guthinger, tells me that it's the superior construction and the attention to detail that has earned French lingerie such a fabulous reputation for being *la crème de la crème.* She says, "We always encourage women to embrace the lace because even when wearing a basic everyday T-shirt bra, the feminine effect of the subtle delicate details on a French bra will come shining through in her attitude, confidence, and positive outlook throughout the day."

Ooh la la.

The Muse of Love

A Frenchwoman will wear beautiful lingerie for herself, not simply for a special occasion or a particular gentleman. She understands the concept of *intention.* If she looks beautiful and knows she is wearing some secret sexy thing under her clothes every day, she will send out a silent message to the world. And the world will respond.

And it's true, if you think sexy thoughts, if you feel sexy, if your bra and panties match (French girls insist on this!), you will bring sexuality and sensuality into your life. It's very much like the muse of happiness. If you are happy and busy, she will visit you often. She wants to be where the party is, where the fun is. It's the same with underwear. If you are wearing lace and silk and some exquisitely frothy panties and bra, then the muse of love will take notice. You will walk down the street with a secret smile, knowing that you have something delicious on underneath. And you will see this beauty reflected in the world around you. In fact, when you go to the market, you will look at the artichokes and notice that they look like lace. The ruffled edges of the red leaf lettuce looks like a Folies Bergère petticoat. And the asparagus looks like . . . well, never mind!

How to Care for Your Lingerie

I noticed the connection between food and lingerie while in Paris this past spring. My French friend Tania took me shopping at her local *marché.* It was a beautiful Saturday morning and she picked out some *saucisson* and *pâte,* a baguette, along with the most luscious strawberries I have ever tasted all for our picnic lunch in the park, as well as some vegetables and a bunch of fresh flowers. As we were leaving the market, I saw some lingerie for sale (yes, they mix and match—clothing, lingerie with fruits and vegetables, wine and cider, flowers and tins of foie gras). I pointed out a pair of pretty pastel panties and matching bra to Tania—they were melon-colored with flower appliqués. Tania shrugged and gave me one of those French looks of subtle disapproval. She told me they were "cheesy." Obvious. Cheap. When we returned to her home, she took me to her bedroom, opened the bureau drawer, and showed me her lingerie. Exquisite. Delicate. I will not give away too many details, but I will tell you this: There was nothing cheap or obvious about these intimate garments. They were sheer and lacy and simple and very, very elegant. She had two or three panties to match each bra. And no, she didn't necessarily buy them at the same time, but she did keep her underthings within a range of particular colors, styles, and fabrics and in this way she always matched. She washes them by hand, with a product you can buy right here in America—good old Woolite! Yes, hand washing delicate lingerie is an evening ritual. In fact, most of the French girls I met have a room that's actually called the "lingerie"—it doesn't mean underwear, but rather a room where delicate things are hand washed and hung up to dry and sometimes ironed. It's surprising to see how many Frenchwomen own an iron and an ironing board. Obviously, they take the care of their most precious outfits very seriously.

Consider getting fitted for your next bra. Lots of good lingerie shops are now providing this service. And if you can't afford to frequent lingerie shops, then consider going to T.J. Maxx or Marshalls or JC Penny or even Target. All of these stores now feature designer lingerie at very low prices. The key to wearing good lingerie on a daily basis (not just for that special occasion) is to buy one bra for every three pairs of panties. Make sure the panties and bra match and, above all, take good care of your lingerie. Oh, and honestly, your husband is not going to complain if he sees your delicates hanging up in the bathroom—or even on the outdoor clothesline. In fact, he'll probably find it very inspirational!

Food and Frills

Later that day, after visiting with Tania, I walked around Paris. I couldn't help thinking again about the connection between the fresh fruits and vegetables and flowers and the lingerie at the *marché* (even though Tania disapproved of the quality). The close proximity of food and lingerie must do something to the Frenchwoman's brain, but I couldn't quite figure it out.

I had just arrived the day before and it was one of the first really hot summery days. The city was alive with the heat and the noise and even the fashion. And the Parisian girls were dressed in their little sundresses and white cotton skirts. There was lots of skin showing. Girls were trying out their new summer sandals. We all had blisters on our feet, but somehow the French girls took out their Band-Aids and happily announced that within a week or so, *il n'y aura pas de problème* (this would not be a problem). Their feet would get used to the new shoes. It was mid-June and the sun didn't really set until after ten at night and so, standing outside the Café Etienne-Marcel with a crowd of loud, chattering, international, very fashionable people felt like something spectacular. It was a Sunday night, which Café Etienne-Marcel had designated as "gay night." Yes, hundreds of men crowded the sidewalks. They were wearing the most adorable summer outfits. Honestly, we could be on Nantucket if you were just to look at the fashion: sherbet colored shorts and polo pony shirts that came in such a fantastic array of colors—pink, blue, green, purple, yellow, orange—that I couldn't help but think of a display I had seen earlier that day, of many-colored *macarons* in the shape of an Eiffel Tower!

Oh, and there are so many pretty women accompanying their gay male friends. Yes, I think the French like to mix it up. And in the middle of all this, the Diesel store across the street had just welded open a window in order to hoist up a tiny Fiat and actually place it inside the store as part of their display. Yes, it was over the top, but it was spectacular. And here we were on a hot night in Paris, spectators at the show.

I sat outside the cafe and watched a girl with black lace on her back. It's some kind of new accessory. Not delicate black lace, but almost a cotton macramé, and I was reminded again of shopping at the *marché* earlier that day and how the vegetables were so beautiful and particularly the enormous artichokes. And then I realized the lace on this girl's back was something like the lace of the artichoke leaves.

And the lace on her back was a little appetizer to what might be hidden underneath her clothes. And so, we've come full circle. If food and sex and love and beauty are all mixed together, how can we not be aware of our bodies, our figures. There's an immediate connection between food and intimacy!

The Lingerie Diet

I honestly believe that this delicious French lingerie satisfies a certain craving for delectable sweets and pastries. I found that walking around Paris and wearing something lacy and luxurious underneath my dress made me appreciate all the gorgeous displays of colorful little round *macarons* at the famous Laudurée tearoom and the chocolates by the artisanal chocolatier Patrick Roger (who, by the way, had a huge block of chocolate carved into the shape of an elephant in his window when I recently visited). And just look at the sexy pastries! There are the delicate details of *profiteroles*, eclairs, pain au chocolat. There's the *langue de chats* (cat's tongue) cookies with a tongue-like shape. There's the *palmiers* (leaf-shaped pastries) and the croissants with their lovely crescent shape. They have the *mille-feuille* (which means "a thousand sheets") made from several layers of puff pastry and the top is drizzled with chocolate and vanilla icing. Oh, and madeleines (little cakes shaped like shells). And finally, there's the brioche, which is more of a bread with an egg wash that looks startling like a breast with a big nipple on top.

It feels as if the entire culture is conspiring to make one feel sexy. And at the very least, this attention to detail and the artistry one can find in food and clothing, architecture and gardens reminds a woman that even the most simple and delicate pleasures should be taken seriously. And with all this serious attention to the details of ordinary life comes a certain kind of happiness—a *joie de vivre*. Because you are not thinking that your ordinary tasks of shopping for the evening's dinner or walking to the post office or purchasing a pair of panties is not important. All of it is important. All of it is the secret to finding happiness.

And if you don't think that buying a pretty bra is a reason for happiness, then ask a woman who has lost her breast.

Love, Loss, and What She Wore

My mother was diagnosed with breast cancer in 1977. I had just returned from a trip to Europe when my roommate gave me the message to call my mother right away. It was urgent. I called to learn that she was in Greenwich Hospital and the surgeons were going to perform a radical mastectomy the following day.

When I was in the sixth grade, my mother missed my violin performance. The doctor had found a lump in her right breast. As it turned out, they removed the lump and found it was benign. But this time was different, and now, her breast was to be removed.

Months after her mastectomy, I went with my mother to meet with a specialist at the Saks Fifth Avenue store on Long Ridge Road in Stamford, Connecticut, where she was fitted for a bra with a prosthesis. Yes, this was my mother—the one with the Frederick's of Hollywood catalogue, the one with the wigs and the black fringe twist dress. And now, she stood behind a little curtain that barely hid her small body and I had to turn away so as not to stare at the hollow curve that now outlined a part of her chest. Her ribs were showing and her stomach now swelled out so that she looked a little like a child. The saleslady helped her with the fitting and my mother chose a very pretty white lace bra. It had a little bow in the center. This little white lace bra made her look even. Normal. And this was everything.

Now, when I think about my mother, I know with all my heart that the right bra, a little lace, some silk, can give a woman a whole world of confidence. And yes, it can make her feel sexy. And sometimes being sexy is no insignificant thing.

We've come a long way since 1977. Having a mastectomy is no longer shameful and hidden. We have marches and walks and reconstructive surgery and implants. I wish my mother could have lived to see this day.

Still, on that afternoon in the Stamford Saks Fifth Avenue store, my mother found her bra and, for a moment, she was happy. So this is the secret then to *joie de vivre:* to love yourself for who you are right now—your beautiful, fragile, imperfect self.

French Lessons

INVEST IN SOME wonderful French lingerie. You can find some in your own hometown or on the Internet. Make sure your bra and panties match—you can do this by buying three panties for every bra. Choose basic black and white and then add to this your third favorite color—red or hot pink or blue. This will help you coordinate your lingerie wardrobe. Within this color range, you can add some fun accessories—slips, stockings with garter belts, and corsets for a retro look. There are also now many stores in the United States that carry stockings that stay up with a strip of clingy plastic that sticks to the thigh.

Remember, anything can be sexy if you want it to be, especially old-fashioned outfits that have a naughty, politically incorrect, vintage feel to them, such as aprons and uniforms and ensembles that are aligned in our imagination with a particular role such as secretary, airline pilot, big game safari hunter, cowboy, or suburban country club doyenne.

Be sure to care for your lingerie by hand washing and hanging up it to dry. Find a special place to keep your delicates organized. And if you can, invest in getting fitted for your bra and some foundation garments. You'll notice the change in your look immediately.

Can wearing well-structured and perfectly fitting undergarments that compliment your individual shape make you feel happier? Yes, absolutely.

CHAPTER ELEVEN

French Dressing

Fashion is not something that exists in dresses only. Fashion is in the sky, in the street, fashion has to do with ideas, the way we live, what is happening.

—COCO CHANEL

MY BEST FRIEND from Bard College, Iris Levy, gave me the boots, her brand-new Frye boots. They were rugged-looking, square-toed, light tan leather boots with a slight platform and a clunky heel. Something a cowboy might wear. She had first loaned them to me and, well, she decided they should be mine to keep. Her mother was furious. They cost almost fifty bucks. A fortune in 1975. But back then we didn't care about money or material goods. And so she wrote a letter just before I left school, saying, "Keep the boots, baby."

I was on my way to JFK to catch a plane for London. My wander year, although nobody actually called it that in those days. It was just something you did after graduation—a kind of MBA for the artsy crowd. The summer before, I had hitched a ride in a van to California at the beginning of the summer. In Los Angeles I worked as a Kelly Girl temp for the Southern California Gas Company. When I had saved enough money, I decided to follow the dream of Haight-Ashbury and I got a ride up to San Francisco, but by the summer of '75 it was full of prematurely aging flower children wandering the streets, their long Mexican peasant dresses now frayed and muddy, seemingly having lost their way home.

But I knew Gregg shorthand and my typing tested at 106 words per minute with hardly any mistakes, so I could always find work. In high school I teetered between the college track and the secretarial track and so in San Francisco, I was able to spend a few months temping for a shipping company in the old Ferry Building. And then, again when I had enough money I left the West Coast, went back east, saved up some more money, and left for England.

I landed at Heathrow Airport at six in the morning in September 1975. London seemed more civilized to me. Safer, anyway. But I was naïve by most standards and all I had was a plane ticket, three hundred dollars in American Express travelers checks, and a backpack containing jeans, my black Danskin top, two Indian-print peasant skirts, a blue-and-white-striped Picasso shirt, an oversize sweater I stole from my brother, a pair of chunky wedged shoes, and some toiletries. Oh, and a Lanz of Salzburg nightgown for those chilly English nights. I was wearing the Frye boots. With only this, I intended to stay a full year.

This wasn't my first trip to London. I had been there the summer before, right after my junior year, when I met a British boy named Alan Driver. He worked as a travel agent in Hampstead Heath. By now, I was in love.

My backpack was actually a large hand-woven basket with

two leather shoulder straps. At JFK, my father had asked me if I was going for a picnic or actually going to Europe.

Here's the thing about Frye boots. They're not all that pretty. They're kind of rugged-looking. Square-toed, with stitching. Back then, they came in only one color—tan. Along with the boots, the store gave the customer a little tin jar of saddle soap and instructions on how to clean your boots, how to care for them, so they would last forever. That, too, was the idea in those days. We raged against conspicuous consumption and planned obsolescence. We lived poor with style. (There was actually a book by this title.) Shopping at the Salvation Army was a political and spiritual decision. Things had personalities—souls, even. We gave new life to old housedresses. We saved silk skirts from the garbage bin. We shopped for vintage at Unique Boutique and Canal Jeans. We bought recycled overalls splattered with paint from the college coop.

Me and Mary Quant

I was on my way to Inverness, Scotland, when someone told me about New York. "It's a ghost town. It's gone bankrupt. They're selling bonds to try to save the city." This was right after the British boyfriend had told me he just wanted "to be friends." I felt heartbroken and lost, but why go back when there was nothing left but a ghost town? So when the money ran out, I found a Canadian temp agency that told me not to worry about the citizenship problem and to just tell employers I was Canadian. I got a job for a dress designer in London's trendy Oxford Circus. The company made a line of very stylish wool coats and dresses. They were simple and well-constructed with big collars and a Mary Quant-inspired trapeze shape. They gave me a burgundy-colored coat that I wore all that winter. It wasn't very warm, but it did make me look like a proper English schoolgirl. The money was not too bad, either, and so after I had saved up just enough, I decided to travel some more. I left London and I took the long and rocky overnight channel crossing to Paris where I met a British girl named Maureen. She came from Ireland and had made this trip many times before because she was working as an au pair in Paris. I was suffering from seasickness and nausea and she was very kind to me and kept me company during the overnight passage. We became friends and she said since I had nowhere to stay in Paris, I could sleep on her floor.

She lived in a five-floor walk-up on the Left Bank—Boulevard Saint-Michel. It was February by then and we kept warm with a little gas heater. (Apparently, it was just as dangerous as it sounds.) And it always ran out of petrol on Saturday night. It was 1976 and someone had invented disco. Maureen would say, "Dancing will keep us warm. Let's go to the disco." We walked out in the cold night air onto Boulevard Saint-Germaine and to Le Cave, where we danced with Moroccan exchange students and boys of dubious backgrounds. I didn't speak enough French and they didn't speak English and so we spoke in a child language. "We make happy?" Yes, well sort of. We kissed on bridges and ate too much pastry.

I walked from the Left Bank every morning, through the Jardin du Luxembourg, over to the Alliance Française. I worked as an au pair, briefly. Mostly, I sat for hours in cafes, smoked Gauloises, and walked and walked and walked. One night I went to a party with real French people at a real French girl's apartment. All I remember is the *shh-shh-shhh* sounds of the French language circling around me and how they were dressed so nicely in skirts and boots and pretty sweaters and how I felt like a ragamuffin in my jeans and Danskin dance top. And the truth was, I had always felt more comfortable dressing nicely. After all, this was what my grandmother had taught me and, in fact, I had made an effort to look like a hippie in castaway clothes. It didn't come naturally. But here I was at a party with elegant French people and I didn't have the words to explain that this hippie get-up was just a pose.

I interviewed for a secretarial job in Paris. It was an English firm—my boss from the dress designer in London set up the interview. I still think about how my life might have played out differently if I had only been a little more patient. I remember taking dictation from a handsome Frenchman who spoke perfect English. I remember sitting down at the electric typewriter, and I remember rolling the paper into the typewriter and securing it under the bar. And then I looked at my shorthand and began typing. Fast. When I finally looked up at the paper, I realized it was riddled with mistakes. I couldn't understand what had happened. And then I looked at the keyboard and realized that the letters were mixed up. It was a European keyboard. The Q was where the A was on an American or British typewriter. And I had to press the capital key in order to type a period. I apologized to the man who had dictated the letter and handed it back to him. He told me he understood the problem and that if I wanted to, I could come into the office and practice. I said I'd think about it, but I never did. I'm not sure why. Perhaps because I was running out of money and needed a job and a real place to stay. Perhaps because I was getting ill. It was February and cold and rainy in Paris and my little British coat didn't really keep me warm. Finally, sick with the flu, I returned to London and temped some more.

Because the Night Belongs to Us

Later in the spring, I arrived in Amsterdam and met up with the same Moroccans I had met in Paris. But suddenly, everyone was gay. I met a red-headed boy from California and he asked me to come with him to hear Patti Smith sing at the Paradiso. It was an enormous cavernous club and she was a speck in the distant light, screaming and chanting—a tiny bird, wearing black. It was hard to tell whether she was a man or a woman. She was mesmerizing and I realized I wanted to be a poet. And I wanted to dress in black and scream and have lots and lots of people come to see me.

By June, I was back in London. I moved into a communal flat in Highgate with a boy from Australia, a girl from Greece, another girl from Canada, and another girl from Vienna—a photographer who had a fellowship at the Central Saint Martins College of Art and Design. Her name was Brigitte and we became fast friends. We both shared a passion for shopping at Biba and the flea market in Kensington and for dressing up in costumes. She took photographs of me, which I still treasure. Aside from all this playing make believe, I slept an awfully lot during this time. My Frye boots sat in the corner of the commune empty, toes curling slightly, calves leaning into each other as if they were conversing, whispering something. The toes were scuffed and stained a dark brown.

Songs from Joni Mitchell's *Blue* echoed in my head in my fevered dream. Then one day, my old British boyfriend arrived and sat at my bedside and I made a miraculous recovery. He got me out of bed and drove us to Cambridge for the day. We had tea and scones and clotted cream at a little cottage by the road.

And then he told me I should go home, back to America.

Bonjour, Tristesse

Whenever I visit Paris, I find myself running into the ghost of my earlier, younger self. She is always on the Boulevard Saint-Germain, right at the intersection of Boulevard Saint-Michel. She is considering sneaking into the Wimpy's for a hamburger and fries. She feels guilty about this, but she is tired of living on cheese and baguettes. She is walking across the Jardin du Luxembourg on her way to the Alliance Française, where she continues to mangle the French language. There is a mix-up in her brain, and it feels as if she is living this half-life. She has forgotten how to speak English correctly. She has forgotten how to type. She has lost her journal at the American Express office. She is afraid of the Turkish toilets. She is tired of sleeping on the floor. She is tired of feeling cold. She would like to take a really hot shower. She would like to have a good meal. She would like to be liked by the French. But the French do not seem to like her, and in fact one day, an elderly French gentleman wearing a suit and tie stops her on the outside the Galeries Lafayette and says something to her in French. When she tells him she doesn't understand and that she's from America, he continues. He asks what she is doing here. He has to repeat the question several times in order for her to understand. Finally, she answers that she's searching for a job and he asks, "Why don't you get a job in your own country?" he asks and again it takes several tries and by the time she fully understands what is being said to her, she feels her face grow hot and red.

Why don't you get a job in your own country? Actually, this is a good question, but it's hard to explain. Nixon had been impeached and New York City was bankrupt. Her mother is in the hospital again and her brother has moved with his young wife to Australia.

The ghost of a girl says none of this, but her clothing speaks for her—saying, "I am a girl from a prosperous country and I am here in my peasant skirt and backpack, pretending to be a gypsy, pretending to have no home."

American Hippies

Not too long ago, my tutor, Marceline, told me that the French—particularly the French of her generation—did not appreciate this influx of seemingly wealthy American kids coming to their country in the late sixties and early seventies. She told me that, in fact, she thought we were insulting the French people. They had endured so much during the war and they had so little and even during the sixties, they were in the middle of a great economic struggle. She told me how when she saw these teenagers and twenty-somethings wearing ripped jeans and old T-shirts and peasant skirts—well, the French saw this as a cruel joke. For them, dressing well—even if you only had one skirt, one dress, one blouse, one little wool jacket, and a nice scarf—was a sign of dignity in the face of hardship. To be well-dressed was a sign that you were not defeated. It was a sign of respect for your family, your neighbors, even your country.

I have not told Marceline that I was one of those hippie girls from America with the peasant skirt and the Frye boots, the Danskin top, the backpack, and the hair in a washer-woman's kerchief. These days, when I visit Paris and I run into my old ghost, I do wonder if she and Marceline had met somewhere by the Cluny La Sorbonne Métro and for a moment, I can imagine myself apologizing to her, wondering if she would forgive me.

Listen to the Grandmothers

To truly understand the roots of contemporary French fashion, it's actually very helpful to observe the French ladies who are now in their eighties. These are the ones who came of age during Coco Chanel's heyday. They threw off the bustles and the corsets, the long flowing skirts, for something simple and classic, luxurious and comfortable. Something they could easily flit about in. These ladies were products of two world wars, during a time when fine fabric was not easy to come by and certainly not inexpensive. When the Second World War broke out, they had to quickly pack up and flee Paris for the outlying provinces. It was an era of great uncertainty. Coco Chanel once said she never wanted to weigh more than a bird on a man's arm. And I wonder if this feeling came from the fact that to be heavy would mean to be a burden—especially in an era when a quick escape might be necessary at any given moment.

With all that said, this eighty-something *femme d'un cer-*

tain âge carries the genome of French style. She is all about being well turned out within the constraints of limited time and money and material goods. (No wonder the scarf is her trademark!) From this fertile environment of lack, plus imagination, we have seen the growth of a style that is highly original, very beautiful, and distinctly French.

Everything Old Is New Again

Still, this idea of doing something imaginative and wonderful with less lives on for today's Frenchwoman. In fact, I first learned of the *vide-grenier* in Auvillar, and later my friends in Paris told me more. The *vide-grenier* literally translates as "emptying the attic." In addition to the regular markets, each village will have at least one special day per year where the townspeople empty out their closets and attics and basements and put things up for sale. It's similar to an American yard sale or tag sale, but it's very well organized and just about everyone in town participates. My friend Tania recently bought a beautiful vintage tablecloth for three euros (a little over three dollars).

Vicki Archer is the author of the gorgeous and visually stunning coffee table book *My French Life* and she's also the creator of the very popular Francophile blog French Essence. Her latest book, by the same name, was released in November of 2010. She's a bit of an expert when it comes to finding treasures and this is what she says about the *vide-grenier:*

> The *vide-grenier* is usually held in open spaces and in my village of Saint-Rémy-de-Provence it is usually in the local car park. The sellers arrive early, set up their trestles, display their goods, and then make

themselves comfortable for what is often a long day. Anything and everything is on display—from antique collectibles to today's unwanted paraphernalia—yet nothing is ever thrown out, and if it doesn't get sold first time it will surely go around again the next. The *vide-grenier* is like a lucky dip; you never know what you will find unless you play . . . and if nothing else, there is always a good lunch to be had. It is France, after all.

What a Girl Needs

Before she even adds the quirky finds she might discover at a *vide-grenier,* the Frenchwoman will start with a basic palette of neutrals, either black or navy or beige or camel, and then she add splashes of color with scarves and jewelry, shoes or boots or gloves. She might wear all black, but add a hot pink cardigan as a form of color blocking. Still, she practices the concept of less is more and because she chooses her basics carefully they last a long time and it seems as if she owns more clothes than she really does.

For an American woman, this system of dressing can actually be easily replicated. First, chose your classic looks carefully and invest in quality fabrics and design. And since these well-made basics are generally not inexpensive, don't spend the money on any of these classic wardrobe components until you find the one that fits you perfectly. You want them to last for a long time. Here's what you'll need:

- The classic white shirt (at least one)
- The pencil skirt (black, navy, camel, white)

- The perfect-fitting jeans
- Several T-shirts or tank tops in black, navy, and white
- The classic little black dress
- A jacket in your favorite neutral shade
- Great-fitting trousers in quality material
- A cashmere sweater (in your favorite neutral shade)
- A cardigan (in your favorite neutral or a complimentary shade)
- The classic trench coat

To this, you can add some fun accessories that show your personality, a little quirkiness, and your imagination. Perhaps your unique accessory is a colorful silk scarf your grandmother gave you or a fun necklace you found at Target. Perhaps it's a pair of hot pink textured leggings you bought in Paris last year. It could be something you bought directly from an artist at a crafts fair. Perhaps it's a pair of killer heels or a pocketbook you found in a consignment shop. The point is, this accessory is something that infuses your own personality into the very basic and minimal classic wardrobe. It's also where you can afford to indulge in a passing fad or this season's hottest look. If you don't spend much on it, it doesn't matter whether it'll look silly twelve months from now.

Next, choose your signature secondary color. Find something that looks particularly great with your coloring. It's helpful to go with a friend and try on scarves. Put them under your chin and decide which colors really bring out your eyes, your hair, and which colors make your complexion glow. Next, think secondary patterns. I personally love the red plaid found in the Royal Stewart tartan. I have a little skirt I bought in Los Angeles in 1993 and still wear it. I consider it my lucky skirt because I met my husband while wearing it! Currently, I am working on bringing leopard print into my wardrobe, but since I'm trying to avoid looking like a "cougar," I've limited my obsession with cat power to a pair of leopard heels and a leopard pocketbook. Okay, that's not completely true. I confess I just purchased a Dana Buchman leopard print coat. It's very light and so sexy and well, I couldn't resist. I actually bought it in a local consignment shop for a song.

So, this is what I mean—you don't have to go to France to get the French look. The secret to the French look is simply about pairing quality basics with unusual finds. *Vide-greniers*, flea markets, and consignment shops are part of the secret. So, how do you cultivate the "eye" for discovering the treasure from the trash when it comes to secondhand shops?

Practice Makes Perfect

It's all about practice. Still, there are some tricks. Most of these shops divide their clothes by colors. So if you've already decided what your basic palette is and what secondary accessory colors look good on you, you can immediately focus in on your particular colors. The next step, before you even pull out a frock or sweater or a pair of pants, is to simply touch the fabric. You can tell a lot by feel. Is it real? Is it man-made? Does it feel luxurious? Does it feel cheap? When you find something in a great color and the fabric feels wonderful and lovely to the touch, then it's time to pull it out and take a closer look.

If all this seems daunting, start with designer consignment shops. They often charge more but are generally easier to navigate. Begin by just hunting for easy things—scarves, purses, gloves. It helps if you have a friend who is a self-styled expert. Still, you can learn a lot by simple observation and frequent visits.

This will get you into the habit of the hunt. And it *is* a hunt, and every visit to a consignment shop will not be successful. Still, you learn something about your style each time you visit. Do you gravitate toward the sheath dresses of the early sixties? Do you love those cinched-waist frocks of the forties and fifties? Do you go crazy for the wild patterns of the eighties? I discovered vintage because I just don't have a contemporary body type. But give me a dress from 1955 and *voilà!* It fits perfectly!

You Are the Star of Your Own Movie

Frenchwomen get their clothing ideas from all sorts of places outside the world of fashion. They are inspired by architecture, films, visits to art galleries, and trips to the aquarium (just think how flashy tropical fish can be in all their glorious colors and patterns). Even food inspires—especially pastry! And they definitely get ensemble ideas from traveling. They search out iconic looks and then build a fantasy. For example, for the western look, they'll have the jeans, the white shirt already, but then our French girl visits Austin, Texas. She must buy a pair of those red cowboy boots! She will wear her jeans and shirt and boots with a little red kerchief around her neck. She'll skip the cowboy hat—too obvious. But you see, there's just enough here to suggest the wonders of the Wild West.

She just saw the latest James Bond movie. She gets out her classic trench coat. Slips on her black pencil skirt. Adds a white blouse, dark glasses, gloves. Boots. And to push it up a notch, perhaps she adds a vintage attaché case—one she "stole" from her dad—and *c'est ça*, she looks like an international spy.

Robin Hood. Honestly, this was the look last fall in practically all the towns and villages I visited in France. I don't think anyone would reference this when talking about fashion, but I saw a combination of thigh-length tunics, wide leather belts worn low around the hips, along with leggings in a variety of colors and colored, floppy suede boots. This was often paired with an over-the-shoulder messenger bag and of course the famous scarf.

Sexy librarian? She'll put on her neutral-colored pencil skirt, matching cashmere sweater, scarf with knot tied to the side, maybe pearls. She'll wear sheer stockings and high-heeled pumps. She'll keep her hair up in a topknot. And she will definitely wear a leather belt cinched around her waist and a pair of brainy eyeglasses. I recently met with Heather Stimmler-Hall, the author of the deliciously sexy (and very helpful!) book *Naughty Paris: A Lady's Guide to the Sexy City.* She met me on rue Monge, wearing a tweed jacket and skirt, a wooly scarf, a fetching beret, stockings, and boots. She was wearing librarian-style eyeglasses and since it was a chilly October night in Paris, she was rather buttoned up. Heather is a slender and very elegant *femme.* She's youthful and quite beautiful and so the layers of clothing, the scarf, the row of little buttons added a delightful sense of mystery. And this made her very sexy!

The Slow Reveal

Yes, the scarf is an important fashion accessory. And this is because you can take a simple palette—a navy dress or a black sweater and a pencil skirt—and then, by adding a belt, some bijoux, textured stockings, and an interesting scarf you can completely transform your look. And you can wear the scarf doubled around your neck or simply draped over one shoulder and fastened with an interesting pin. Oh, and if it gets chilly, your large scarf can double as a shawl. Scarves are magical accessories and the French know this more than any other culture. Yes, a scarf can keep you warm in the winter. It can be tied and wrapped in endless combinations. If you feel bad about your neck à la Nora Ephron, it's the perfect solution for *une femme d'un certain âge.* There is something incredibly classy about wearing a scarf and it can add the finishing touch to just about every outfit.

But more than this, the scarf is so sexy! Men are crazy about women wearing scarves because when you think about it, the scarf is a kind of seductive prop. Say you meet a man in a café, you sit down. It's cold at first, and so you keep your scarf on. Perhaps you slowly remove your gloves. After a while, you warm up and so you loosen your scarf. Just a titch. Just enough to reveal the curve of your neck. And then, after a time, you slowly untie, unravel, and pull the scarf from your neck, like a delicious striptease. This tying and untying and wrapping and unwrapping drives a man crazy. In some ways, it's sexier than actually undressing because it's so restrained and yet makes him imagine what it would be like to completely and truly undress you. You see, by wearing layers, you create intrigue, you complicate things, and well, this is extremely provocative.

The Trick Is to Care

I noticed something while sitting in a cafe in Toulouse. The women were dressed to please men. It was really okay. In America, I think we sometimes have difficulty with this idea. For a number of years I worked in script development at Paramount Pictures for the actress Meg Ryan. Lots of writers, directors, and producers would come into our offices to pitch story ideas. You might think that someone who wants to make a big Hollywood movie would dress very well indeed, but actually no, not at all. In fact, it was considered very *uncool* to dress up and so most of these movie folks made an effort to look like they had made no effort at all—they wore jeans and sneakers and wrinkled shirts or black T-shirts and baseball caps. This was the basic uniform. And I suppose it's the American way. We have casual Fridays and we like the idea that we are not imprisoned by a uniform. We are free to be comfortable. But still, I wonder if this is just another method of conforming? And then when it's time to dress up, we go all out and perhaps overboard in the other direction and we lose our sense of balance.

Back at my cafe table in Toulouse, I noticed that Frenchwomen will wear something simple—the skirt and blouse—but then they add some charming accessory and a belt that matches their scarf, or an amusing pin. They aren't ashamed of looking as if they did make an effort. They *did* think about what they'd be wearing today. No, it's not overdone and it's not too matchy-matchy, but there's a sense that she knows men are watching and she likes to please. Is there something wrong with dressing to please? I don't think so. Wouldn't the world be a better place if we all made a little effort to please our friends, our family, and our community by wearing something that's attractive?

Once Upon a Time

The fabulous artist and watercolorist, Francophile, and creator of the blog Paris Breakfasts, Carol Gillotte, says red is an important color for Frenchwomen and she traces it back to the fascination with *Little Red Riding Hood* and *Alice in Wonderland.*

> Hardly anyone wears red in New York City, but you'll see it all over Paris. Frenchwomen will wear just a bright red scarf to cheer up a rainy, gray Parisian day, but you can also find them in head-to-toe red. Grannies will wear red and young children will wear red shoes. Marc Jacobs the designer actually made a red wedding coat. Red slips, of course. Sometimes you'll see a little edge of red showing from under their jackets.

Oh, and have you seen the Christian Louboutin red-sole shoes? Now there's a great example of how a sudden glimpse of bright red viewed from beneath a woman's elegant black pump can create a sensation and a whole new look. That's the power of the color red.

Along with red, you might find splashes of hot pink. And then there's that beautiful Hermès-inspired orange. Recently I saw some electric blues and yellows in France. The point is, the French aren't afraid to add a splash of vivid even startling color and neither should you be! Still, if you want to be *trés Française*, start with red!

French or Not French (the New Cafe Game)

Micheline the image consultant told me that she often likes to spend a Sunday afternoon sitting in a café with a friend in the center of Paris, observing other Parisians. "At a glance, we notice or can guess who is Parisian and who is not. It's a real pleasure to do this exercise." Micheline is a wonderful observer of women and indeed, she helps newly transplanted British and American businessmen and women navigate through the French way of life. She has a trained eye and tells me that much of what she has learned comes from the ancient art of observation.

I recently tried out my own version of this game at a cafe on the Right Bank. I sat at a table with another American and we tried to guess who was French and who was not French. It's not as easy as it may sound, because there are a lot of Francophiles running around Paris wearing scarves and striped Picasso shirts and pretty skirts and boots and doing their very best to pass as French! (Yes, that would be *moi.*)

Still, there are subtle differences. The main way you can tell the *French* from the *not French* is more than the fact that the French look well-planned and that they look like they actually made a little effort when they got dressed that morning. There's always one little thing that is unique to each Frenchwoman, something original and eye-catching. It might be a lacy forest green camisole that is peaking out from beneath a tailored jacket. Or it might be sandals that show off rainbow-painted toenails. (My friend Tania did this with the pastel shades I brought for her from America. Each toenail was painted a different color!) This original touch could also be an accessory—like a bicycle that Suzy, a young Parisian art student, has painted in red and yellow stripes. You see, while there's a certain look and a way of dressing for show, for theater—it's also important to create your own signature style.

You Are Beautiful

So, this little original something is actually at the heart of French style. It's beyond the boots, the scarves, the perfectly fitted jeans, the high heels, and the classic trench coat. It's this little secret ingredient that is yours and yours alone. But, in truth, it's powerful and potent, because to really employ this secret ingredient—well, it's like recognizing the power of your own ruby slippers. Sure, they were on your feet all this time, but did you know they had the power to ward off bad witches and that they could transport you from one land to another?

It's all about confidence. Once you discover this thing that is yours, then it's yours forever and it makes you strong and it makes you beautiful because you have finally learned to love who you are right now.

Shopping with Sylvie

Sylvie took me shopping. Yes, this fifty-six-year-old Weight Watcher agreed to go clothes shopping with a slender thirty-something Parisian woman. A beautiful girl with great style. Sylvie frequents a particular series of boutiques in the Fifth Arrondissement and so she received a special discount and wanted to share this with me. Before even entering the boutique, I decided I would only look at bags and shoes and I would not even attempt to try on any clothes. I imagined that they wouldn't have anything in my size—a French 48—anyway.

Well, to my surprise, they did have my size. And in fact, there were women in the store—Frenchwomen—who were just as big as me. And while I tried to stay in the background, Sylvie produced a couple of skirts and some dresses for me to try on. Honestly, I did not want to do this, but at the same time, I did not want to seem like a bad friend. After all, this was a great opportunity and she wanted to share her discount with me. And so, I tried on several things. The saleslady joined in, suggesting this top or this skirt or belt to go with the outfits. Now, I'm normally very suspicious of a saleslady who starts suggesting more items, but this woman was really good. Together, she and Sylvie offered some wonderful additions and I found myself actually enjoying shopping. They chose a beautiful long, lacy skirt for me, and then an Ungaro dress in a clingy tan fabric. The dress was originally one hundred euros. With Sylvie's discount, I would be able to buy it for half of that. Yes, an Ungaro dress for fifty euros or around eighty dollars. It was a summer dress with little puffed short sleeves and a ruched bodice that included four little heart-shaped metallic buttons. The dress had a 1920s feel to it. It was very feminine and flowing with a sash that went around the hips and tied on one side. On one sleeve, there was a little rhinestone heart. Ungaro is famous for dressing women such as Penélope Cruz, Catherine Zeta-Jones, and Sharon

Stone. He's all about being sensual. And if you go to his website, you will learn that he "embellishes everyday garments and reminds women that they are the joy of every man."

And so, I went behind the flimsy dressing room curtain, took off my skirt and top, and put the dress over my head, pulling it down over my body. It did fit—but then it was a clingy material and so I supposed it could fit anyone! I came out and presented myself to the waiting saleslady and to Sylvie. They gasped. They smiled. They said, *"Oh, oui, bien sûr!"* This is the dress for you!

Still, I felt very skeptical about this.

And, in fact, I looked at myself in the mirror and all I could see was two enormous breasts and a huge amount of cleavage. I would never wear this dress. Everything was showing—the hips, the stomach, the derriere, and the breasts. Two of them. Big ones. But here I was, in Paris, and these two delicate Frenchwomen were squealing "*ooh la la,*" that I looked great and that I had to buy this dress.

Honestly, I thought maybe they were secretly making fun of me. Maybe this was some crazy French joke and I was just not getting it. Ha ha ha. I told Sylvie I would never wear something that's so—*fitted.* "Why?" she asked.

"Because of my size," I whispered.

Then she told me that when I wear such loose clothing, I am not making myself look smaller or sexier. I am just hiding. "This dress shows you off," she announced firmly.

And then she reminded me that to have *joie de vivre* means having a positive outlook on life, to enjoy the moment, a certain lightness of being, to feel great and happy with yourself—to have *être bien dans sa peau*!

So, I bought the dress.

The Dreams That You Dare to Dream

Yes, I bought the dress. I bought the dress because there was one tiny part of me that thought, Perhaps she's right. Perhaps I do look good in this dress. And anyway, an authentic French girl—a *Parisian*—picked it out for me. It was part of my experience, a souvenir from a Paris shopping experience. I had no choice but to buy it.

Later, in Sylvie's apartment, she told me that the French adore big women and then she showed me videos of the American singer Beth Ditto. Beth Ditto is truly a big gal, but you can see her fans adore her. I began to process this. But even after I returned to America, I was still not sure, till I learned that the June 2010 issue of French *Glamour* has a big fashion spread about plus-size models. Oh, and they are so cute, so adorable and sexy and French and well, voluptuous.

When I got home, I did a little research and found that as incredible as it might seem, the whole perception of weight is changing in France! There's a new understanding that all women are not meant to be skinny and that women with curves are actually considered sexy. I even found a fashion spread that Karl Lagerfeld and *V* magazine recently created for Chanel in the famous atelier at 31 rue Cambon, featuring the beautiful and very, very voluptuous burlesque star Dirty Martini wearing Chanel lingerie and little else! Apparently, this fashion spread was a form of apologia from Lagerfeld, who had once declared "nobody wants to see curvy women."

And I recently talked to one Frenchwoman who told me that France is having the same kind of body image discussions that we're having in the States, and things are rapidly evolving. And, in fact, a law has just been voted on that makes it mandatory for pictures of models in magazines to have a warning that the pictures have been altered or photoshopped. Not too long ago, Dove made a big impact when it came out in France with advertising promoting all kinds of beauty and real bodies. There's even a television show in France called *Belle Toute Nue* (*Beautiful Naked*), which helps overweight women learn to love their bodies. You see, for the French, this idea of *être bien dans sa peau* (being comfortable in your own skin) trumps everything. And so, even if you do need to lose some weight, first you have to be comfortable in your body and love your body as it is right now, in this very moment.

My friend Margie directed me to a video of Luce, a very talented nineteen-year-old singer who was one of the winners of *Nouvelle Star 2010,* France's equivalent show to *American Idol.* I watched a YouTube video of Luce singing "Somewhere Over the Rainbow."

In the video, Luce wore a big blue bow in her red hair, blue stockings, a hot pink dress, and a bright yellow belt. She sang the song with a Caribbean beat and it was a showstopper. I sat at my desk and found myself crying. And then the judges had their moment and when the only female judge—a very slender, very stylish *femme d'un certain âge*—told Luce how wonderful she is and she started to cry—well then, I cried some more.

And in that moment, I couldn't help but think about my French grandmother and imagine myself as a twenty-something girl wishing that perhaps somewhere over the rainbow dreams that you dream really do come true. What if she had lived to see this? And for me, I think I have spent the last thirty years fighting my own body, gaining then losing, then gaining again, always in a perpetual state of unrest, unhappiness. Never feeling *être bien dans sa peau.* Oh, what I would give to be able to tell that younger version of myself, "You are beautiful. Exactly how you are right now." And since I can't tell her, I will instead remind myself of the words my French friend Isabelle told me and I will find comfort:

> And even when you feel down, sorry for yourself and miserable, tired or pessimistic, it is about still keeping a tiny flame within you that says nurturingly, tenderly, like a good parent to a child: "It's okay, you will be fine; all that pain and sorrow will move away at some stage. Life is *still* beautiful. Believe it. Relax into it. What could you do now that would make you feel a little bit better with yourself?" Even if it is a tiny thing, like calling a friend, taking a bath, lighting a candle, or putting on a nice movie, do it. *Joie de vivre* is tightly linked to self-confidence and self-esteem. If one did not have the chance to grow up as a child with an environment allowing this healthy self-love to blossom like a flower, well, one has to trust that he/she can always work on it and retrieve her rights to self-love and self-confidence. It is slow, patient work, but it pays back in the end. I compare self-development to the image of climbing a mountain: it will always go up, but the more you train yourself and climb that mountain, the more you gain strength, muscles, wisdom. So sooner or later you will recognize the paths that need to be avoided,

> you will choose the easier ones; you can find helpful people along your way that can take your hand for a few miles or more (friends, strangers, partners, therapists, healers). And the cherry on top of the cake, as we say in France *("cerise sur le gâteau")*, is that the more you climb, the more beautiful the sightseeing is when you turn around and look at the view.

And so today, I am taking baby steps. I am climbing up the hill. I am admiring the view. I am daring to dream my dreams.

And yes, I am wearing the Ungaro dress. Okay, only in my own backyard, but it's a beginning.

French Lessons

BEGIN BY LOVING YOUR body just as it is right now. Dare to dream and dare to be beautiful.

Start collecting quality basics—skirts, a classic black dress, a white shirt, great-fitting jeans, a beautiful cardigan. Choose your neutral color—black, navy, cream, or gray—and then accessorize with splashes of color, bijoux, and signature items such as a vintage brooch. Discover your own consignment shop and frequent it often. Once you get to know it, it'll be easier to find not only quirky items, but also overlooked classics and designer clothes.

Let go of things that are cluttering up your closet or are just not right for you anymore. Bring them to the Goodwill or the Salvation Army. Or if they are just too precious, give them to your daughter or niece or a good friend. You'll discover how handing something precious down to someone else can bring both of you a whole lot of *joie de vivre.*

Dress up. Consider the fact that you are making an impression on people. By dressing with a sense of style and a sense of history, you are honoring your friends, your family, and your community. Dressing well builds confidence and self-esteem. Be inspired by the world around you—by art, cinema, travel, food, and grandmothers. Oh, and read classic and contemporary books with intriguing heroines. Find your "type"(Audrey Hepburn, Marilyn Monroe, Angelina Jolie, Madame Curie, Michelle Obama, Carla Bruni, Princess Grace), think in terms of iconic style and begin to live as the star of this movie called your life.

CHAPTER TWELVE

The Real Voyage

The real voyage of discovery consists not in seeking new landscapes, but in having new eyes.

—MARCEL PROUST

YES, I RETURNED HOME from France changed. To the casual eye my change might have appeared rather superficial—I had a new dress, a pair of adorable belle epoque-style boots. Lingerie, *bien sûr.* Lots of little bottles of lavender crème de cassis from Toulouse to make lavender kirs. I knew a little more French. I had lost five pounds (which was actually a surprise, considering all the baguettes, fresh butter, *macarons,* croissants, foie gras, wine . . . I could go on!).

But the truth is, I hadn't changed in any obvious way.

All during my journeys, I was searching out the secret to happiness. *Joie de vivre.* And I thought this search would help me to get skinny, learn to speak fluent French, and learn to cook really, really well, transforming me so that I would be stylish, gorgeous, fabulously French and happy!

I walked into our house and greeted my husband. He was happy to see me, but also happy that I had gone to France.

I confess, I was actually a little annoyed that he was so happy. I suppose I imagined he should be slightly upset by my absence. But no, he was thrilled for me. (And of course, the goodies I brought home—the wine and the chocolate and the collection of lingerie—certainly added to his thrill.)

It took a few days after my return, but I realized that there was nothing wrong with my husband not being upset and actually being glad for my travels. After all, I am fifty-six years old. I am married to an open-hearted man. My daughter is twenty-six, grown and about to get married. My father is healthy and has a girlfriend. And you know what? I am free.

For the first time in my life, there is no one who truly needs me to be around all the time to care for them. This was an amazing realization, because as women, I think we all suffer from this overwrought sense of obligation—to constantly care, to tend, to nurture. But then sometimes we forget how to nurture ourselves.

And so, I realized it's my turn. And I am free to create my own life.

La Belle France was the key for me. Just like Dorothy in *The Wizard of Oz*, it took a trip to a faraway land to come to the realization that there's no place like home. That's the secret to happiness, the secret to *joie de vivre*. It's about finding those moments in your own ordinary life, finding the people and the simple pleasures of living, that will bring you happiness. And if it means traveling to France to finally come to find happiness in your own backyard, well, that's good, too!

Happiness doesn't come from one big thing, but rather, it comes from sparkling little moments that are strung together like the beads in a necklace. One moment follows another and then another and another. Each moment of your life—whether it's from the serenity of sitting in the shade in front of your hometown library or the thrill you get from running in the Boston Marathon or the joy you get from petting a little orange tabby kitten—every experience teaches you something about who you are and where your personal *joie de vivre* lives.

(Oh, and yes, upon returning from France I did adopt an orange kitten from our local shelter! *Bonjour,* Mister Pickles!)

The Glass Half-Filled

Still, you might wonder, How do I locate my own *joie de vivre*? I suggest you start first by shifting the way you think. Consider becoming a wild optimist. My father used to sing this song from the 1940s—"Ac-Cent-Tchu-Ate the Positive." I love this song because its message is so clear. Be optimistic. Seek out what is good in this world and in your life.

When I question my father about whether I should take on a certain project or not, he will ask me, "Is it fun?" Yes, he believes that this is what counts. And as silly as it may seem, this is actually very sound advice. It's hard to really stay with something over the long term if you don't find it fun. And if it's not fun, you just won't put your whole heart into it. So, yes—something may be difficult and strenuous and hard work, but if you have fun doing it, well, it won't seem like work at all. I used to think that my father was a little naïve, but honestly, the older I get, the wiser my father gets!

Amazing, huh?

Clouds in My Coffee

I had this thought this morning as I was making my coffee back on Cape Cod. I have a very complicated procedure for making coffee, so let me describe it to you: First I take out my special cafe au lait cup. This cup was a gift from my daughter. She went to a Color Me Mine pottery store and painted it. (It's one of those fun places where they give you the pottery and the paints and brushes and sponges and then you paint a design. Afterwards, you leave it there and they bake and glaze it and then you can pick it up when it's ready.) This cup is very special to me. My daughter's signature is on the bottom of it. It is celadon green and has a big yellow flower painted on the inside. Back to my coffee—this is how I like to make it: I heat up two-thirds of a cup of nonfat milk and then I put two tablespoons of ground espresso in a Melitta filter and then place this on top of the cup. But because this is a large cafe au lait cup and the filter is small, I must put two knives on top to keep the Melitta filter balanced on top. And then I pour boiling water into the coffee in the filter. I've been doing this for years. Some people have asked me why don't I get a cup with a smaller mouth or why don't I get a bigger Melitta filter or why don't I just buy an electric coffeemaker or get a French press? I don't know, really. I guess I just like my little ritual.

Generally, I feel a little apologetic about it, a little embarrassed. But when I returned from France, I thought, Suppose I saw a Frenchwoman doing this strange coffee ritual? Would I say, "Oh, she's crazy"? No. I would think, My goodness, this is so interesting. So exotic. I would be very accepting. I would probably write about it in a book!

All this is to say, who we are and what we do is often a matter of perception. If you can step back and look at yourself through the eyes of someone else—a foreigner, perhaps—you might find that you are a little kinder, a little more forgiving of your own quirky personality, your foibles, those things that make you uniquely you. I do believe that when we look at our hometown through the eyes of a tourist, that when we stop a moment to appreciate our lives—and indeed love our lives—we will find our *joie de vivre*. Our happiness.

Perhaps this appreciation for *joie de vivre* is so prevalent in France because it's a small country and it's easier to travel to a foreign place and then come back with new eyes and a fresh appreciation for home. Or perhaps it's easier for the French to find new things among the treasured old things. Perhaps it's because France has been an occupied country and her citizens have known hunger and loss of freedom in recent history. Or perhaps it's because France is an agricultural country and her people are so close to the land, whether they live in the country or the city. Yes, we are very different, but it seems to me there are lots of lessons to be learned from our French sisters. First, let's try to make it a point to get out and go someplace new and different. We don't have to take a cruise to Patagonia. How about just visiting a nearby town that you've never been to? How about switching up your daily routine? How about taking a day to pretend you're a tourist in your own town? The point is to look at your own world with new eyes. When you do this, you will find your love of living—not just love for the place or person that is exotic to you, but love and appreciation for what you have now in your own life.

Or how about simply taking a day for yourself. Enjoy a minivacation in your own Secret Garden. Marjorie my friend in Northern France, believes in taking time for herself, although this did not always come naturally for her. Here's what she recently told me about the nature of happiness:

> What I think *joie de vivre* is—perhaps it is the real and true knowledge that we do not live forever, and should not pretend that we do, or expect to. While I am glad that I can be such a young fifty-eight, I also am aware that I am not immortal. There is a time and place for everything, and without death, life would not be a story, because a story has an ending. . . . There is an expression in French that does not exist in English: "*changer les idées*." It doesn't mean "change your mind." It means get off somewhere and abandon all the stuff that's running through your head for something different—take a break, really take a break. Just forget it. Live for now. Vacation trumps everything. I used to find this annoying. Now I am happy whenever I have a day off. I used to need to be moving ahead with work, or whatever. Now I can be thrilled with a day of gardening before me, or a hot bath, every morning in spring, getting up and going outside and taking in every little change that takes place in the garden.
>
> Also, I recently realized that, at my age, it makes absolutely no sense to be a "glass half-empty" type of person. There just isn't enough time left. I need to add up every half glass I can get, and savor it.

Daddy's Girl

This term has never described me. I was never very close to my father growing up. He traveled a lot and well, my mother claimed me as her own and actually kept us apart (that's a story for another day). I was part of what she dubbed the "Girls' Team" and my brother and my father were on the "Boys' Team." I grew up in a very girly-girly way, where fashion and makeup and dancing and theater and dinners out were the most important things in the world. When my father was away, we ate ice cream for dinner and stayed up to watch old black-and-white movies on *The Late Late Show.* I didn't know about the outdoors, really. I didn't go on the camping or the canoe trips with my father and my brother. I didn't learn to tie knots or change the oil in the car.

And then in 1997, my mother died. And I truly "met" my father for the first time. I will never forget standing in the parking lot outside the hospice in Branford, Connecticut, and looking at my father, shaking his hand, as if we were strangers and thrown together for the first time. We were awkward with each other, but we couldn't let this stand in our way. There was a lot to do. A eulogy to write. Funeral arrangements to make.

Today, my father and I are very good friends. We are still tentative with each other. We are still very polite with one another. It's a fragile but deeply poignant and precious relationship.

I visited my father at his home in Connecticut last week. He had just bought—now don't get scared—a chain saw. Yes, he had cut down an enormous tree in his backyard that had fallen during a late-summer storm. His neighbor helped him (thank goodness!).

My father wanted to show me how he was now sawing the fallen tree into enormous hunks from which he planned to make chopping blocks and even a table or two. I followed my father into the backyard, crunching through the fallen leaves.

It was chilly and in the air was the possibility of snow. I stood patiently as he pointed out the various piles of wood and I nodded my head as he told me how he had organized all of it. Truthfully, I was slightly bored. All this wood. And then there was the little "fort" he built out of the rocks he'd removed. He'd taken up knot tying lately, just to keep in practice. I was thinking about going out to lunch, but then as I stood there, listening to him explain to me that this was an oak tree and the wood has a particular color and pattern, suddenly a new thought emerged and it was this: My father is a foreign country. This backyard, this wood, these leaves and trees, his aged flannel jacket, his white beard and twinkling green-blue eyes—this is all part of *his* country. And this place where he resides has its own language and rituals and food and fashion. It has its own music and educational system and philosophy. The point is, I found myself suddenly fascinated by my father. I love this country! It's so different from my country!

And there, in this very ordinary moment—nestled beneath the wood chips and the piles of oak leaves, hidden somewhere in the green grass—I found *joie de vivre.*

Yes, it was there all along, but somehow I had to travel to France and return to finally see it. Still, it was worth the wait. *Bonjour,* Happiness!

French Lessons

HAPPINESS DOESN'T COME FROM one giant leap—say, from winning the lottery (that brings its own struggles), but rather, happiness comes from taking baby steps that will lead you to your own personal bliss.

Consider making a commitment to someone else—whether it's your husband or partner. Agree to take partner dance classes together. Or join Weight Watchers and promise yourself to make at least one new friend. Volunteer to help out at an animal shelter or an organic farm or your town's art festival.

Next, give to yourself. Truly give. Give yourself a break. It's okay to spend a Saturday in bed every now and then. Honor that and enjoy it. Be patient with yourself and recognize the need to retreat to your Secret Garden. Find ways to bring sustenance and ways to nurture your mind, your heart, your body, and your spirit. Find what brings you joy, what makes you laugh or smile. A place that "fills you up" and from which you feel replenished and happy to be alive. This is your own personal wellspring.

Create a rhythm and a pattern in your life so that you can easily visit this wellspring on a regular basis. Find friends within this wellspring. Cultivate your friendships like the flowers in your garden, so that when the day comes when you lose your footing, the friends within your wellspring will be there to lend you a hand and bring you back into your group, because yes, happiness is sweetest when it's shared.

Acknowledgments

FIRST AND FOREMOST, I thank all the Frenchwomen who opened their doors and hearts to me. This project would not have been possible without their generosity. I thank them all—and a big *merci beaucoup* goes out to Marceline Colton, Sylvie Gourlet, Tania Fovart, Isabelle Avril, Béatrice Le Nir, Marie Joëlle Bévalot, and Micheline Tanguy.

I give a big, hearty heaping of thanks to my American friends—living here and in France—Marjorie Van Halteren, Jessica Lee, Paula Martin, Elizabeth Gold, Nancy Flavin, Deborah Davis, Carol Merriman, Amy Handelsman, Susan Kuntz, Brenda Horrigan, Alex Crowley, Laurie Graff, Deb Krainin, Lisa Solod, Beverly Aker, and the brilliant Debra Ollivier!

I am so grateful to be working with amazing sister Francophiles—my editor, Audrey LaFehr; my agent, Irene Goodman; and my publicist, Maureen Cuddy and all the good people at Kensington!

I thank all the fabulous Francophile bloggers who encouraged and inspired me with all their brilliant and beautiful writing and pictures—Paris Breakfasts, La Belette Rouge, Polly-Vous Français, and French Essence (just to name a few!).

I am particularly indebted to the Virginia Center for the Creative Arts for awarding me an international fellowship to stay in Auvillar, France, and to the Massachusetts Cultural Council for awarding me a life-changing artists fellowship for my fiction.

I thank Cheryl Fortier and John Alexander for making my time at VCCA / Auvillar so delightful! I thank MediaBistro and the Grub Street writers organization for all their support and for all the wonderful students I've been honored to meet.

I thank my daughter for always being a style icon and an inspiration.

I thank my husband for his encouragement and his fabulous cooking!

I thank my dad for teaching me how to find joy in ordinary things.